First in the Family

ADVICE ABOUT COLLEGE FROM FIRST-GENERATION STUDENTS

Your College Years

BY KATHLEEN CUSHMAN

NEXT GENERATION PRESS

Providence, Rhode Island

This volume is the sequel to *First in the Family: Your High School Years* (Next Generation Press, 2005, $8.95), in which the authors of this book describe how they made their way to college admission, offering practical strategies for others to do the same. Both volumes are available through online booksellers; for orders in quantity of ten or more, please contact the publisher at info@nextgenerationpress.org.

———————

Next Generation Press
P.O. Box 603252
Providence, RI 02906
www.nextgenerationpress.org

ISBN 0-9762706-6-8

Please visit www.firstinthefamily.org for more information and resources about first-generation college access and success.

Book design by Sandra Delany

10 9 8 7 6 5 4 3 2 1

Acknowledgments

Generous support for this book came from Lumina Foundation for Education. The opinions expressed here are those of the authors and do not necessarily represent official policies or positions of Lumina Foundation for Education.

Abe Louise Young deserves enormous credit for her help in developing this volume. She arranged student interviews and conducted two of them, and, in the final writing stages, she provided essential editorial guidance. Irina Feygina and Celia Bohannon also contributed significantly to the work of organizing the student voices presented here, and Rosa Fernández helped develop the worksheets and appendixes. Montana Miller gave generously of her expertise throughout the interviewing process. As the book's photography editor, Barbara Cervone brought in images that could reflect the power of these students' experiences.

Next Generation Press owes its greatest thanks to the college students whose insights and advice make up the substance of this book. They came to us with the assistance of the following people and organizations: Dr. Mamta Motwani Accapadi at the University of Texas in Austin; Patty Chong-Delon at City College of San Francisco; Pete Coser at Oklahoma State University; Bjorn Danielson at the Center for Native Education at Antioch University in Seattle; Chris Douse at Indiana/Purdue University at Fort Wayne; Jennifer Frank at the Community College of Denver; John Hilley and Anderson Williams at Community IMPACT in Nashville; Dr. Virginia Jane Rosser at Bowling Green State University in Ohio; Darrick Smith at Oakland Technical Arts High School; Irene Sterling at the Paterson Education Fund; and the Rural Schools and Community Trust.

Contents

Introduction

When you pick up this book, you are finished with high school for good—in fact, it may be already long in your past. You have a new goal now, a harder one: to get yourself through college and earn the degree that can change your life.

You can think in a new way about your learning now. In this mindset, grades and deadlines continue to matter, but your education no longer feels like a race with an end. Instead, it's a continuing journey of discovery.

All during your college years, you will be finding your way to your dream. You'll have hard work to do on this journey: thinking through difficult material, writing well, asking questions that push you further. But you will acquire new tools that help you to do that work, and meet experts who will teach you to use them.

Not just the work but the relationships you forge in college make you stronger, smarter, and wiser. Getting to know other students, you will dig into the challenges of academic learning and increase your understanding of the diverse world that awaits you. Forming ties with your professors, you will discover new fields of study, new ways of thinking about the world.

Your degree will bring many rewards—partly because you can expect to earn more as a college graduate. Its most important rewards, however, come from the qualities you will be developing: independence, initiative, confidence, and self-direction on your path through life.

Whether you attend a private four-year college, a state university, or the local community college, you have much to learn from others who have gone before you. In this book, students like you lend a hand along your college journey. They share their experiences, offer their guidance, and give you some practical tools for getting where you want to go. We hope that their conversation will open up possibilities for you and encourage you when you need it most. Each one of them has learned so much in college—about themselves, and about the larger world. Now it's your turn!

You're on your way

College is a journey of discovery

*E*ric Polk sat in the front seat of the car that was taking him away to college and tried to make sense of the mixed emotions he felt. Behind the wheel was his mentor, John, a community leader who had helped him come the distance from the poorest section of Nashville, Tennessee, to college acceptance at Wake Forest University. A few hours before, Eric had said goodbye to his mother and grandmother, his favorite teacher, his old friends from the neighborhood. He was pulling away from them now, yet at the same time carrying them with him.

He remembered every one of his struggles to become the first in his family to attend college. Yes, he was proud and excited—but why did he feel such a knot in his stomach?

>> I started thinking about all the highs and all the lows, and just seeing my life flash by. And it felt like a long journey to freedom. Like, man, I'm leaving everything behind that was challenging me, that didn't want me to be here, or that pushed me or pulled me to get here. It was like, "I'm on my way!" I was anxious, I was nervous, I was excited, I was scared! = ERIC

When you get the news that you are accepted to college, you have every reason to celebrate. You are also striking out into new territory, however, especially if no one in your family has gone before you. Any explorer feels the excitement and the worry that Eric describes, at the beginning of a journey of discovery. In the pages that follow, other students tell how they crossed the bridge into their college years.

Remember why you're going to college.

You already know that your college degree can make a big difference to the life you will lead in the future. You may not have decided what you want to do with your education, but you have plenty of reasons to get it.

Mike Morris came from rural Mississippi and felt deep loyalty to the aunt who had raised him. He struggled with academics, but Brigham Young University in Utah offered him an athletic scholarship. Mike went off to college far from home, in a place where he often felt like a stranger. Even when a football injury put him on the bench, he kept his eyes on the degree that could lift his family out of poverty.

» I'm in college for them—to better them, give them a chance. As long as I can get my aunt her first house, her first own land, and help my cousin out with her child, I'm happy. - MIKE

Debra Graves worked from the time she was a teenager to support her young sons as a single mother. For her, starting community college near her home in Denver was a chance to have people take her seriously. Through the mayor's office, she received a grant to study in a field that interested her.

» I saw this quote, "God provides food for the birds, but he doesn't throw it in the nest." That, to me, means everything. Dreams are out there waiting for me, but I've got to do the work to make them happen. If I want my children to be successful, I don't leave that in someone else's hands. If I want to do well in school, then I'm the one responsible for it. That's what drives me. - DEBRA

You'll need good guides to help you through.

Like many other students in this book, you might have had help from others as you decided to apply to college and gained your admission. Now you are on your way, but during what lies ahead, you will need even more support.

Aileen Rosario is in college because she wants to be a lawyer. In Paterson, New Jersey, her family struggled with hard times, and her high school counselors discouraged her from college. But her supervisors at a nonprofit education group—who once were first-generation students, too—took her ambition seriously. Aileen has now finished two years at her local community college and is enrolled in a state university. She still works at the same place, and her employers still stand behind her.

>> They said, "You could do it, you just have to go to school for it!" That's when I started thinking about the options I had, and I started researching it. I consider them my parents in a way. When I have a problem and I come to them, they understand me and help me fix it. – AILEEN

Such assistance might come from your community or from the people you meet at college. Wherever you find it, that support can help you make important decisions and adjustments throughout the years ahead. Keep your eyes open from the start for the people who reach out to you. They will be your guides through unfamiliar territory.

College is about change and discovery.

As you get to know more about your choices at college, you may start to discover new interests and develop in new directions. You could change your ideas of who you are and what your future might hold. Those close to you might understand and support your new ideas, or maybe you will feel their disapproval.

Stephen Torres grew up, the son of a barber, in a Mexican-American neighborhood near Austin, Texas. An excellent math student in high school, he attended a summer course at the University of Texas that introduced minority students to the field of engineering. When he won a scholarship and began his first year at the university, everybody thought he would go on to be an engineer. But as he became involved in Latino groups on campus, his interests turned to politics.

>> I thought, "Wow, this is college, so let me get a little understanding of what it really has to offer." I love engineering, but when I really realized how much my identity and my background meant to me, I changed my major to Mexican-American Studies. I didn't want to sit by myself in an engineering bubble, stuck on that side of campus among the same people. I could do a lot more by working to define policy-making for urban and rural school districts, and things like that. – STEPHEN

When you start college, you bring along not just your own hopes and expectations, but also those of your family and others who care about you. Your former teachers may already picture you on a certain career path. Your family might expect you to keep helping out in the ways you did before. Your romantic partner may expect to stay together, or you might have children who need your attention.

Perhaps everybody assumes that you will return to your old neighborhood after you finish college. Niema Jordan comes from Oakland, California, and grew up with economic struggle. Her mother works as a security guard and her stepfather drives a bus; neither one went past high school. But Niema has a passion for writing, so she worked hard to get into the journalism school at Northwestern University, outside of Chicago. She might go back to Oakland, but she knows she will not be living in the projects.

» I embrace my life and how I was raised. It's me, it's where I come from, and it has molded my outlook on so many things. But it's not going to be my life as an adult. I know that already. I'm destined for something better.
– NIEMA

College is your time to discover new possibilities, meet new people, test new ideas, develop new skills, and make new connections. The time and energy you put into the next several years will earn you a degree, if you work hard and keep at it. But college can also help you grow and learn in ways you cannot yet imagine.

» In high school I saw college as something you do so that you can move on. All you've got to do is get this degree—this piece of paper—and get a good job and make some money and have a family and do great things with your life, if you want to. And there's so much more. – STEPHEN

During his years at college, Stephen began thinking deeply about his Latino identity and his values. He shaped his studies, and his future, around his beliefs about politics and community. For him, the purpose of college was no longer simply to rise in the world—it was to change the world.

Your background gives you extra strengths.

You may feel uncertain about where you fit in at college, especially if most of the other students have more economic privilege. When she arrived at Northwestern, Niema saw many contrasts between herself and her classmates. But as her first year went on, she also started to see the positive edge that her tough Oakland upbringing gave her.

She knew how to handle herself in a city like Chicago, whereas a lot of her classmates had no clue. In her journalism class, she could get stories that others were afraid to go near—interviews with people living in housing projects or on the streets. And she could live on very little money.

>> Most college students don't have enough money to go out and do whatever it is they want to do. And if you come from a background where there's been penny pinching, you know how to handle that. The struggles we've gone through have prepared me for my life as a college student, and also prepared me for my future career. In some ways it gives me a bonus.
   – NIEMA

Not only that, but her own experiences could educate and enlighten others, Niema realized. She had fought an uphill battle to get to college and that gave her plenty of muscle. Her fellow students saw that and they often came to her for advice.

>> People in college have breakdowns—it happens. And a lot of times they'll come to you for help, because they see that strength that you built up through whatever difficult and chaotic struggles you had. They're like, "Wow, how are you so strong?" – NIEMA

As a minority student who came from a rough part of Cleveland, Raja Fattah knew that he stood out on the largely white campus of Kent State University in Ohio. But he saw that as an advantage, especially with his major in justice studies.

>> In our country right now, it gives you an edge automatically, because our country is not just white Anglo-Saxon Americans like in the 1800s! It's diversified. I'm Palestinian, so I had a foundation set for Arabic. – RAJA

Raja decided to make the most of his family's native language by taking more courses in Arabic language. Combining that with a degree in justice studies, he would stand a better chance of achieving his dream, to work for the F.B.I.

You can *build* your education—not just receive it.

Like Raja, you won't be sitting back passively to take what others arrange for you in the next four years. You had to push hard to get where you are. Now you can use what you know about life to stand up for yourself, shape your own education, and take what you need from college.

» Middle-class Americans who are college-educated have all this power. But even though people are in college, they're ignorant to a lot of things. They don't know where I've come from—there are people here who never heard of Oakland, who went to public schools that were the greatest things on earth. So why should they make choices for me? Going to college, you have access. You can tell people what's going on. - NIEMA

Even though Stephen grew up only a few miles from the University of Texas, when he arrived on campus as a first-year student, it did not feel like home to him. At first, he felt like a second-class citizen there.

» White students, with parents who came to this university, expect to be listened to. Whether their work merits that respect or that attention, they expect it—and generally what you expect out of life, you're going to get. Your circumstances are going to affect your life. Let's not pretend like they don't. - STEPHEN

Then Stephen began to form connections with other Latino students. His confidence grew as he helped organize events that brought them together—and also educated the larger community about Latino issues.

» As much as I didn't want to admit it, I was in fact political on this campus, by nature of my skin tone and my last name. And if you can empower a student, we can definitely move on to bigger and better things. I want to tell new students, "You have a voice, use it. You have a brain, use it." There's so much you can learn, and if you expect people to listen to you, they will. - STEPHEN

Because you are the first in your family to go to college, many challenges lie ahead of you—personal, academic, and financial. But as you step out into your new life, remember that you have already proved that you can meet a challenge. The intelligence and skills that got you to college will only grow stronger as you use them.

WHAT ARE YOU TAKING WITH YOU?

As you prepare to start college, think back on some of the challenges you have met so far. Later, you can use this list to remind you of your strengths and skills.

A personal challenge I faced:

_____

_____

What I did to meet it:

_____

_____

An academic challenge I faced:

_____

_____

What I did to meet it:

_____

_____

A financial challenge I faced:

_____

_____

What I did to meet it:

_____

_____

WHO STANDS BEHIND YOU?

Different people—perhaps a special teacher, mentor, or friend—have probably helped you get to this point of starting out for college. When you arrive, those people will continue to be interested in how it goes—and they will want to support you when you need it. Use this space to write down contact information for the ones you really counted on, so you can keep in touch.

Name _____

Email _____ Phone _____

Address _____

_____

Name _____

Email _____ Phone _____

Address _____

_____

Name _____

Email _____ Phone _____

Address _____

_____

Name _____

Email _____ Phone _____

Address _____

_____

Name _____

Email _____ Phone _____

Address _____

_____

Name _____

Email _____ Phone _____

Address _____

_____

Name _____

Email _____ Phone _____

Address _____

_____

2

Facing the Hurdles

College can be a culture shock

Milenny Then grew up in a Latino neighborhood of New York City, its busy streets in the shadow of the George Washington Bridge. As a teenager she dreamed of leaving the city to explore new places. But her parents, immigrants from the Dominican Republic, wanted to keep their only daughter close to home. When she got a scholarship to Wheaton, a small college in suburban Massachusetts, they told her she was crazy to think of going so far away.

>> It's just in the culture—I'm the only girl, so they are kind of overprotective. They wanted me to go to college, but I should stay at home, where they have control over what I do. But I've always been a rebel. – MILENNY

When she arrived at college, however, Milenny realized that she had new bridges to cross. Coming from an urban high school with fewer than ten white students, she was joining a largely white student body accustomed to privilege and status. She had left her alternative public high school knowing that she could do hard work well, but after her first few weeks of class, her confidence was shaken.

>> It was really hard for me at first. I never cried because I was homesick in college—the only reason I cried was because I felt dumb. One night I called my cousin and I was like, "I feel so stupid, I shouldn't be here." – MILENNY

Milenny got through that period partly because she decided she would prove that she could. She relied on the qualities that had brought her this far already—self-reliance and an openness to new experiences. When she felt discouraged, she followed her instinct that things would get better in time.

>> If you think about it too much, you really won't do it, because all those "ifs" get in the way of what you really want to do. – MILENNY

Many first-generation college students face the hurdles Milenny did, during the first few months of college. They feel the tensions of leaving home for new territory, and their parents cannot reassure them. The people at college seem like a club of insiders, to which they do not belong.

As they describe those initial feelings in the pages that follow, remember that all of these students made it past that first stage—and so will you.

Expect tensions at home as you begin your college years.

All through his high school years, Eric's mother had stuck by him in his efforts to get to college. But in the last few weeks before he left, it seemed that she and Eric were always arguing about something. When his departure day came, she sat in her car with her arms crossed. His other family members did not come to see him off.

>> Like she didn't think the day was coming. I was mad, at her and at the others—they could have at least said goodbye. – ERIC

Thinking back on their quarrels, Eric realized how hard it was for his mother to let him leave home.

>> I kept saying, "Hey, in three weeks you don't have to deal with me, in two weeks I'm going to be gone, I'm leaving in a week!" And the last time I said it, she's like, "Have you ever realized that maybe I *need* you here?" I was like, "Whoa, why would you want me to be here, where I would be a burden to you?" – ERIC

Not everyone moves away from home to go to college, as Eric and Milenny did. But whether you go across the country or across town, it's normal to feel tensions with the people who will not take part in your new life. They are happy for you, but at the same time, they know that you are going somewhere outside their own world. They may not be able to put that feeling into words, but it can threaten their sense of well-being and their desire to protect you.

Aileen's parents knew she wanted a law career, and they were proud when she got into the John Jay College of Criminal Justice. The summer before she started, she took evening classes there to prepare her for college writing. But the college was an hour's bus ride away in New York City, and Aileen could not arrive back at the bus station in New Jersey until after midnight. Her parents put their foot down.

» I really did like the school, I enjoyed everything about going there. But they worried that something would happen to me—that's why they moved out of New York in the first place. They said, "You're not going back, pick another college." I was seventeen, so I had to do what they told me to. I didn't have time to pick another college, so I just went to the community college, where the only thing I had to do was register for classes. I figure I'll do my bachelors here, in New Jersey, and then after that I can just go for my masters over there. — AILEEN

Two years later, Aileen did graduate from community college, and transferred to the nearby state college. When she finishes there, she still intends to go back to John Jay—this time, for her advanced degree.

Not just family members but also friends who do not go on to college may feel left behind. Hazel Jansen started taking community college classes while she was still finishing high school in Denver. Her boyfriend objected when she no longer had time for him.

» He would get mad when I told him, "No, I can't drive over to see you tonight, I'm really tired and I have to get up early in the morning for school." – HAZEL

Before, people might have depended on you to fill a need for them—whether it was the money you earned, the help you gave, or just the pleasure of your company. Now those important contributions may have to change, if you are to make the most of your time in college.

You can acknowledge the different feelings that everyone is having, and recognize that you will miss each other. But you don't need to take any blame for going on to college.

By getting your college degree, you do something good for yourself—and you also contribute to your family and community. In his first year away at college, for example, Eric began to study sociology. Instead of worrying about the distance between him and his mother, he was already imagining the ways he could work to change his old neighborhood for the better.

Arriving at college can be a culture shock.

You might be headed for a community college around the corner, where many other students share your background. But if you go to a state or private university, your fellow students may not seem to have much in common with you. Jackie Comminello worried about this when she started at the University of Colorado in Denver.

» I was so nervous going in there, because all these white people were dressed nice and I could tell they had money, they probably went to really good schools, and I knew it. I was like, Wow, these people are really smart and here I am coming from North High School. So I was intimidated, I felt like I wasn't going to do good. But I decided to stick it out, just go against the odds. – JACKIE

Eric felt similar worries when he first arrived at Wake Forest University, a selective private college in North Carolina. Students were driving up in expensive cars packed with stuff to outfit their dorm rooms. The clothes they wore looked nothing like his. From the minute he opened his mouth, Eric realized that he spoke differently.

» When I first came, I used a lot of slang. But some of the stuff that I can say and do at home—like "Yo, what's up, pimp?"—I can't do it here. They just looked at me real funny, like, "What did you just call me?!" So I've calmed down a lot of my street slang: You can't say this, watch how you say that. Because that's too much of a culture shock for *them*. – ERIC

Eric had discovered that he actually knew two languages, which would be an asset to him as he moved through his different communities. He didn't have to give up his neighborhood style, but he could choose the times he wanted to use it and when he would speak more formal English.

When Mike left Mississippi for Brigham Young University, he found himself in a conservative Utah setting. The college rules frowned upon the kind of social life he used to enjoy in his rural African-American neighborhood. People even raised their eyebrows at the way he looked.

» I have tattoos on my shoulders—one that says "love family" in Chinese writing, one of a football, and my initial. And people around here don't believe in that. – MIKE

During her first months at Northwestern University in the Chicago suburb of Evanston, Niema had a hard time with its quiet setting. It made a sharp contrast with where she grew up.

》 I was trying to understand how these people could have such perfect lives, like out of the suburbs, and people in Oakland could be struggling the way they were. – NIEMA

When she went out with friends to formal dances on campus, she felt out of place.

》 I can't call my mom and ask her necessarily what to wear. She's never been to those type of events, she's like, "What are you talking about?" – NIEMA

But as Niema got off campus more, she discovered that this college town had more than one side to it.

》 Evanston is one of those places that's really split up. It has poverty, there's students who are struggling. You get this off-kilter idea of it, because you don't necessarily have to leave the campus if you don't want to. – NIEMA

Exploring the edges of Evanston helped Niema feel less alienated. Just as important, she began to see that her first impressions would not always reveal the whole story about a place—or about a person, either.

Milenny, too, saw that her first assumptions did not always hold true. When she later became a residential adviser in a dormitory, she grew more attuned to the complexity of her college community.

》 I learned not to assume, because I had to deal with so many people. Even just making a bulletin board, I couldn't assume that everyone was a certain religion or a certain race. How to interact with people became very important. – MILENNY

Stick it out, and keep connecting with people.

In the sea of faces that met her during the first weeks at college, Milenny didn't understand why a particular staff member approached her and suggested they meet to talk.

>> I said okay, but I didn't know why, at first. But she just really wanted to help advise me—help me pick my classes, know who to talk to if I had a problem. She was just trying to guide me through. - MILENNY

Milenny began to realize that help like this could get her through the culture shock, the academic stress, and the uncomfortable new environment.

>> If I could get help from twenty people, I would go see the twenty people! I think that's what made me different. - MILENNY

In the chapters that follow, you will hear other students describe in more detail how they managed to go after their college education while staying true to themselves. Your first challenge now is to get your feet on the ground and point yourself in the right direction.

PEOPLE TO GO TO FOR HELP

On this list, keep the names and contact information for college officials who can help you with the "business end" of your college years. Not every college has the same offices, so the ones here are just examples and you can revise or add to them. Keep the list in a convenient place so you can use it when you need to troubleshoot problems.

OFFICE	CONTACT NAME	EMAIL	PHONE
Financial aid office			
Admissions office			
Dean of students			
Multicultural office			
Academic counseling			
Writing center			
Tutoring services			
Career services office			
Housing office			
Dorm advisor			
Health services			
Counseling services			
Office to address discrimination issues			
Disability resource center			
Athletic office			
Transportation information			
Campus police			

3

It's Your Time

Take charge of your academic choices

*Y*ou can get into some major trouble within a couple of hours in the rough section of Cleveland, Ohio where Raja Fattah spent his high school years. Raja's parents are Palestinian immigrants. The vocational high school he attended did not challenge him much, and few of its students went on to college. But Raja and three friends decided they would all apply to Kent State University, an hour's drive away. They stuck together for support on Kent's enormous campus with its 30,000 students.

Raja's father wanted him to study business in college, but his first few courses in that field did not interest him. His criminal justice class, on the other hand, began to answer a lot of the questions he used to have when harassed by the cops.

>> If I'm going to college for four years, I want to be interested for the time I'm there. I want to learn things that I haven't ever been introduced to before. I stuck with justice studies, so I would never get bored. – RAJA

Raja recognized that college presented him with a chance that might come only once in a lifetime. For four years, he could explore, ask questions, and think hard about what mattered to him. Even more than high grades, he went after the goal of opening and sharpening his mind. Whatever career he chose, he would graduate with the skills to take on all kinds of challenges.

As a first-generation student, college is your time to find yourself in your learning. In the following pages, Raja and others tell how they did that.

Choose courses that match your level and move you forward.

As you decide which courses to take first, try to accurately and honestly assess your current skills. During the four years ahead, you will get the chance to take thirty or forty courses. It's worth your time now to build a really solid foundation, so you'll be ready for all the new interests you'll want to study later.

Raja took a hard look at his high school preparation as soon as he got to campus.

>> I didn't really learn anything from high school. When I entered college, I just basically started from scratch. In Cleveland public schools, you probably learn more about street smarts than book smarts. It was fun and I was second in my class. But I would say we were cheated out of a good education at that school. – RAJA

Karen Powless started at a state university in Oklahoma, many years after she graduated from high school and became a mother. Taking remedial classes gave her more confidence about joining the academic scene.

>> I went in there with the idea, "I had so many years out, and I know I'm rusty, math and English is not my best thing. But if I want to be a successful student, I'm going to have to brush up. Maybe I'll learn something I've never learned before." There has to be a little bit of humbleness there, because we're not all study-minded. So I didn't feel bad taking basic math or Comp 1. You hold your head up, because at least you're doing it! – KAREN

Naixing Lei came to San Francisco at sixteen from China, speaking no English. He graduated from high school and enrolled in community college classes, but he knew his limited English would make his progress more difficult. So he shopped around for the classes best suited for students like him.

>> On the very first day I go to the class, I sit there and take a look at my surroundings. If I find that every student looks like American-born, I know maybe this class is going to be heavy, difficult, because they all speak English. I pick another course instead. – NAIXING

During his first year, Naixing found a writing course tailored for English language learners. Later he grew more comfortable participating in classes that demanded more fluency in his new language.

On the other hand, you may find that you are more advanced than other students in certain subjects.

>> I didn't speak formal Arabic, I spoke colloquial Arabic. So when I got to college, I took a couple Arabic language classes, and I'm still taking them. And it's expanded my whole language in Arabic, so more people from the Arab world can understand me, no matter where they're from. – RAJA

Look for courses where the teaching style meets your needs.

Raja needed more of his classes to draw him in and motivate him somehow, as his language classes did. In his first two years, he had several disappointing experiences in large impersonal lecture courses.

>> I got bored with the whole experience. I've had intro classes with 800, 900 people. The professors are not going to remember my face, they're not going to remember my name, and my grades dropped because of that. When I finally got into my major, my grades started picking up. The classes become smaller, and a teacher will notice you if you come or not. Teachers start opening up to you, they tell you about their experiences. – RAJA

Your college courses will expose you to many different teaching styles. You won't always get a choice—for example, most majors require at least one large introductory lecture course. But you can balance out your course load so that you are always taking something that works well for you. Here are some of the possibilities:

- A very large lecture where the professor delivers information and students take notes, with no time allowed for questions

- A "section meeting," where a teaching assistant works with a smaller group of students who are enrolled in a large lecture class

- A smaller lecture, where the professor mostly talks but also asks and answers some questions of students

- A laboratory where students work in small groups to conduct scientific investigations, with the professor or teaching assistant acting as their coach

- A discussion seminar, where up to twenty students discuss the assigned reading or writing with each other and the professor

In addition, different college teachers will use different methods to see how much you have learned and to decide what grade you will get. Some possibilities:

- Several tests and a final exam using short-answer and multiple-choice questions

- Tests that require written answers of a paragraph or more, and a final exam that asks for one or more short essays

- Several shorter papers and one long final paper instead of a final exam

- A final project (perhaps culminating in writing a paper, giving an oral presentation, or building a website)

- A take-home or open-book final exam

Sometimes several different teachers will be teaching the same course at different days or times. It's worth trying to get one whose approach matches the way in which you work best.

Network with others to find the best teachers.

At the University of Colorado in Denver, Jackie tended to get very anxious when she took tests, even if she knew the material. Also, she was very concerned about her grade point average, because she wanted to get into a selective dental studies program. So she asked other students to suggest professors whose approach would help her with those concerns.

》 Some of my professors would give us extra credit questions on our exams. That not only helped to relieve my test-taking stress, but also gave some leeway for my grade. And I look for professors who give homework and exams throughout the course. That way, you're studying a smaller amount of material at a time, instead of cramming nine chapters into one huge exam. – JACKIE

Karen also networked with other students at Oklahoma State to get their recommendations for good teachers.

>> Basically, it's word of mouth: "Who did you take for government, who's good for Comp 2?" Otherwise the counselors just put you in a class with a schedule that fits. – KAREN

Because he was still learning English, Naixing looked for teachers who spoke clearly and were willing to explain things that he did not understand. When he found them, his language skills improved and so did his grades.

>> Sometimes the teacher is just talking to talk, and is not willing to answer your questions. Or they talk really quickly, and when they write something on the board it's messy, hard to see. The primary reason that helped me gain an A was a teacher who explained everything very patiently and with details, so I can understand and absorb the lecture very easily. – NAIXING

The first week of class is a great time to "shop" for teachers that inspire you. If they don't, move quickly to replace that class with a better fit. Don't worry about offending the professor by doing so; it happens all the time.

>> You can drop the class. You don't have to take that teacher, you can take the class with somebody else. – RAJA

Eric found out too late that the teaching style of his math professor did not work well for him. He had done well in high school math, but in his first semester at Wake Forest University, he got an F in his course in probability and statistics.

>> I thought I had lost my math gene! So I went to talk to a friend of mine and he gave me all the direction that I needed. He told me, "This a hard school, but it's not about what class you take, it's about *who* you take." He also told me that if you fail a course, you can retake it the next semester and take the better grade. The next semester, I took the same math with another teacher, and I got a C. – ERIC

On the other hand, if you stick it out with a teacher, you may be glad that you did. Debra felt humiliated when a teacher criticized her first paper in public. But she swallowed her pride, went for help, and gave herself time to find out what else the class might hold. By the end of the course, she was earning top grades.

>> You'll be surprised at the end of the semester to see that you didn't just learn how to write, you didn't just learn chapter one in your psychology book, but that you learned so many other things from your peers, from the instructors, that are outside what's in that textbook. – DEBRA

Go for courses that you *want* to take, even if they take you in new directions.

Naixing went to City College of San Francisco hoping to transfer to a four-year college and go on for a career in business. He signed up for classes like math, which could help him achieve those goals. But he decided to take other courses, like art, just because they would take him in interesting new directions. His favorite course, Asian-American Studies, connected to both his personal history and his future.

>> To understand better the current Asian-American community, I need to study their past. I felt deeply interested in their struggles and their story. It was a lecture course and every Friday we watched a movie about their past. We saw how not just Chinese but Japanese and Koreans came here—their obstacles, their different roles from the 1840s to the present. There are many misunderstandings and conflicts between people from the East and the West because they only have limited knowledge about the other group's culture and tradition. – NAIXING

Having a strong interest in a subject makes it much more likely that you will do well in a course, even if it is hard. Eric had always loved to read and write, but after his placement test, the college put him in a first-semester class that would provide extra support in those skills. He began earning good grades in it, and so he cautiously asked his professor if she thought he could handle two writing-intensive seminars at once during the next semester.

>> And she looked at me really funny, and she's like, "I think you would be awesome." I'm like, "Will you write me a letter of recommendation?" She's like, "Honey, I will do better than that, I will go talk to the people myself." – ERIC

When she was eighteen years old, Debra flunked out during her first semester at the Community College of Denver, because she thought "it was all about having fun." Six years later she went back, because she wanted a better job to support her children. But her motivation wasn't only financial.

>> I also wanted to know things. I didn't want to know just the little box I lived in. I wanted to know what happens outside, how things work, things that were important to me and my community. I wanted to know how the political system works in my community, even to build my vocabulary so that I can write a grant. So it started out with me needing to improve my education, but now I feel so much more empowered with the knowledge I've gained. – DEBRA

First-generation students, especially, may feel pressure from home to choose courses that suit their families' expectations about the purpose of college.

>> When I went to college, my family was like, "What are you going to study, what are you going to do when you graduate?" And later I realized it doesn't really matter that you decide before you go. Just go, and take different subjects to see what you like. Because a high school class in history is very different from the way it is in college. – MILENNY

Maly Fung's mother, a Chinese immigrant, wanted at least one of her three children to become a doctor or a lawyer in America. But Maly decided to major in international affairs.

>> I still don't know how to say "international affairs" in Chinese. I say, "You know, Mom, it's government, it's history, it's economics." She says, "Oooh, economics! Good, good!" She is never discouraging, but she always says, "What are you going to do with that?" – MALY

Raja just didn't care that much about what he was learning in his business classes. He decided that if he studied a field that had more attraction for him, he could always use what he learned to go into business later.

>> You either buy something or you sell something, that's how business always goes. In my first two intro classes, I got an A and a B and I didn't even try. But it felt like just something to go to, like all my other classes. – RAJA

Remember that this is your time to explore.

As soon as Raja began to follow his own interests in choosing courses, he enjoyed his studies more.

>> Some teachers require you to go find readings in scholarly journals, and I had never heard of scholarly journals coming out of high school. You find articles on things I never even knew existed, everything from death penalty issues, discrimination laws, all types of things. It really expands your horizons. – RAJA

At the same time, he felt his academic muscles getting stronger with practice.

>> I challenge myself—I take upper division classes when I don't even have to, just to get a higher learning experience. – RAJA

Rena Priest didn't know what she wanted to do when she first started at Northwest Indian College, on the Lummi reservation where she grew up. But she had loved working on her high school plays, so she tried majoring in theatre.

>> I spent my whole first year just grinding away, not feeling like I was getting anywhere with it. Then I took an English class, and it was just a perfect fit, it was like finding a groove and then clicking in it. That's all you really can do—just go and try, and keep trying, keep trying. You're accomplishing something the whole time, even if it doesn't seem like it. – RENA

Your college education can be all about developing yourself in the ways that Raja and Rena describe. As you pick up new skills and content knowledge, you will also be learning new things about yourself. Remember, this is your time to grow and change.

In the next chapter, students will tell how the relationships they formed with college teachers, mentors, and friends made a difference to that growth and learning, and helped them on their way.

MY COURSE SELECTION WORKSHEET

As you look through the course catalog and talk to friends and advisers, use the worksheets below to organize the classes you select each term. (You can copy the blank form and keep using it throughout your time at college.)

What courses I might take during Term _____ Year _____

Because I need extra help in this area	Because the college requires it for graduation	Because my major requires It	Because I am interested, even though it's not required

What courses I might take during Term _____ Year _____

Because I need extra help in this area	Because the college requires it for graduation	Because my major requires it	Because I am interested, even though it's not required

MY PATHWAY THROUGH COLLEGE

As you think about what you should study and what your future might hold, it sometimes helps to "plan backward" from a career you think might interest you. You can copy this worksheet and use it to try out lots of different possibilities. Start by filling in a career you can imagine yourself in. Then sketch out the courses, major field, summer experiences, scholarships or fellowships, and people that could support you in that direction. If you don't know the answers, take this sheet to the college's career services office, to somebody who teaches in a related academic department, or both. They can help you design a pathway that will make the most of your time in college.

Possible career:

_____

Possible major(s) that could lead to this career:

_____

_____

_____

Possible related courses:

_____

_____

_____

Possible things to do in summer to prepare for this goal:

_____

_____

_____

Graduate school required for this career (if any):

_____

_____

_____

Sources of financial support (fellowships, etc.):

_____

_____

_____

People to consult about this:

_____

_____

_____

My questions and notes about this pathway:

_____

_____

_____

_____

_____

_____

_____

Enlarging Your Circle

Make relationships that help you do well

John Berry grew up in a small Indiana town, where almost nobody went on to college. He graduated from high school surrounded by farms and fields, and by other people who planned to stay in town and work as their parents did. John held down factory and maintenance jobs for a while, but soon he got bored and restless. He decided to go after a future in which he could use his mind as well as his hands.

When John enrolled at Indiana University–Purdue University in Fort Wayne, he knew he needed plenty of help to earn his degree in history. His high school education had not prepared him for the difficult reading, writing, and math that college required. But he had learned in the work world that good relationships with others could make all the difference in his advancement. John drew upon his outgoing nature to talk to the people he met, build relationships, and get a lot of advice and feedback—enough to launch him to a whole new level of learning.

>> That's what I've really developed here, is a social network. Through student government, I sat on committees with top administrators. When you get to know people in the upper-level administration beyond their title, there's a lot you have in common. The vice-chancellor and I share the same drive to see minority students succeed. She told me, "If you ever need anything, my door is open." - JOHN

By his senior year, John had such good grades that he could plan to go on for a Ph.D. in history. And he also had great references from the people who had come to know him well—professors, college administrators, and student leaders with whom he had worked closely. In this chapter, students tell how they reached out to others, forming a social network that mattered both personally and academically. If you enlarge your circle as they suggest, those friends and connections can have an impact not just during college, but for the rest of your life.

Start with your faculty adviser (and change if it's not a good match).

Your college will assign you a faculty or staff adviser, who is supposed to help you choose the right courses for your level, your hopes, and your expectations. Contact that person right from the start, and make regular appointments to check in together.

>> My college adviser helped students in so many ways, whether it was about having trouble adapting to college life or about filling out a form. She would always be there to listen and help. Mentoring, explaining to students what to expect next, how to navigate through campus life. That's what a good adviser does, gives lots of support. So seeking out those people, wherever you are going to school, that's really key, and then being willing to take their help and their suggestions. – RENA

Let your adviser know where you're coming from academically. When Aileen started community college in New Jersey, her counselor helped figure out how to fill in the gaps in her high school education.

>> He saw that I was really doing something with my life, so he helped me set up my schedules in order to graduate in a certain time. Some people stay in community college three or four years, because they don't know what they have to do. But I was determined that I wanted to spend no more than two years in that college. When my counselor found out I was bilingual, he had me take the CLEP exam in Spanish. I got a high score, and that gave me twelve more credits toward my degree. – AILEEN

If you aren't getting the help you need from your adviser, you can switch to someone else. Jackie Comminello began college at a four-year state university, but she found the most understanding counselors when she took her placement tests at the community college next door.

>> For dentistry, you have to do high levels of chemistry, physics, biology— and I had never had any of these subjects in high school, so it was all new to me. At the community college, they found out more about the students, their background, what type of classes they've had to prepare them. So I went into a smaller biology class there, which was a lot easier for me to learn in. – JACKIE

Debra also went knocking from door to door, until she found the right advisers for the questions she had.

» Often it's the third or fourth person that gives you the help you are looking for, and they will appreciate all of the effort you went through to find them. And not asking can sometimes have hard consequences. You may be one or two years into school thinking you know what you are doing, only to find that you're on the wrong track, you're in the wrong degree program, you could have finished a lot sooner if you'd done the same thing in a different track. Don't put your future in someone else's hands. – DEBRA

Build relationships with professors.

College offers you a wonderful opportunity to have conversations about ideas with professors who have gone deeply into their particular field. If you leave it to chance, however, it may not happen. Stephanie Serda's sociology course took place in a big lecture hall at Bowling Green State University, and the professor couldn't possibly know the names of most students. But Stephanie and her friends would sometimes see him sitting by himself in the student union, and one day they decided to say hello.

» We went over and talked to him, and it was pretty cool just meeting and getting to know the professor. Because obviously sociology is something that's not technical—you can just talk about people, you know. We went back and talked to him a couple other times in the semester. He definitely liked it, and now he knew our names too. – STEPHANIE

Stephanie had realized one of the great advantages of getting to know your professors: They can give you new insights into the subjects the class is about. Nowhere else in their lives do most people have the chance to explore ideas in dialogue with people who have made learning their life's work.

You might even develop a new academic interest just because you find a professor who is passionate about the subject. Milenny decided on a whim to learn Italian, after she watched "The Godfather" on TV. From the first class she took, her Italian professors inspired and encouraged her.

» There are a lot of similarities between Italian culture and my Dominican culture, and that was interesting to me. And the language was so beautiful. So I just stuck with it, and that's what I learned the most in. My professors encouraged me to do internships to practice my Italian, and they always tried to help me when they saw me struggling with my essays. It's the one class that when I do work for it, I don't feel like I'm doing work. I love it.
– MILENNY

When she tried her first class in Italian, Milenny never imagined that she would end up double-majoring in the language, spending a semester in Italy, and thinking of being an Italian teacher herself. With every new class in the subject that she took, her world grew larger.

Relationships with professors can also turn into important friendships. You could discover a similar background or a shared interest, for example. Or your teacher might simply appreciate your commitment to learning, and reach out to you on a personal level.

» I didn't learn about the Holocaust until sophomore year in college. So I'm sitting in the class and I'm reading about the Holocaust, and just digesting all this literature. It's not easy to do. After class I went to my mentor—she was a Christian who converted to Judaism. I broke down crying: "How could this happen, I don't understand, and it was so recently..." She was there for me, she sat down with me, we ended up talking for an hour. That kind of relationship, it's hard to find, but it's wonderful to have.
– MALY

» I had a human anthropology class my second year, and I lost my textbook. So I went to ask the professor if she had any extra material that I can read from while I buy another textbook. And she gave me her textbook! I knew from there that she wanted me to learn. – RAJA

How do you get to the point where a professor knows who you are and cares about your progress? In the following sections, students spell out the steps they took to get those important relationships under way.

Go to every class.

First-generation students who succeed in college say that one key move—going to all their classes—gives them a huge advantage. And if they don't, their grades suffer.

» It really is kind of a domino effect: If you don't go to class you're going to do bad in one class. If you're trying to catch up in that, you end up doing bad in the next class. If you're taking five classes, they're all going to roll over, and you'll end up getting maybe one A or a B in one of those classes, and you're getting Cs and maybe Ds in the others. – RAJA

» Everyone else is skipping class, it's like, "Oh, might as well." And my mom's not saying, "It's time to get up for school." But if you don't go to class, you can't get good grades. For me it was a learning experience, to not do good that semester. – STEPHANIE

Aileen has made getting to class a rule she never breaks, even if she feels like sleeping late.

» I don't miss a class just to be home or hang out with somebody. I don't miss a class unless it's an emergency. Even when I'm like, "Oh, I'm so tired," I just get up and go to school. Just get it over with, every single day. You really have to have a determination, 'cause if you don't have that, what else is going to push you to do it? – AILEEN

Some students think they shouldn't go to class if they haven't done all the reading—that they might embarrass themselves if called on in class. (We'll discuss how to handle a heavy reading load in Chapter 6.) But it's not true. Even if you can't get through all the reading, you can gain knowledge and understanding by paying attention in class—and have stimulating discussions. Being in class also helps you identify your questions and gives you important time to think about the material.

» You have to be in that class, because you lose so much if you miss lectures. Sure, maybe you can get the notes from a student, but you're not hearing the lecture firsthand. You miss the opportunity to ask questions. – KAREN

>> To get that A, you have to be in class every day, you have to participate in the discussions, you have to take it seriously, find out what you want to get out of it before the class starts. Anyone can do it. But it's not high school. You are paying for these classes. Show up. Everything you miss, you're going to need. – DEBRA

Visit your professors during their office hours.

A good way to build relationships is to go see professors during their office hours.

>> That's probably the best way that you can let a teacher know that you want to learn and you're in class. If you have any real valid questions, ask a question. Some teachers honestly don't want to be bothered, but some love when you come to their office hours. They're sitting in their office for an hour, and sometimes no students show up. And they kind of get bored, and they figure everybody's learning. But that's never the case. – RAJA

Many students have trouble approaching their professors for help. The gap between professor and student somehow feels too great to bridge. But you're not the only one who doesn't understand everything covered in class.

>> I just feel a little intimidated, like it's going to feel really weird to approach them. Maybe I'll ask a question that they'll think is ridiculous. If I'm going about something that is really complicated to me, I don't want them to think, "Well, maybe she's not right for this class." – JACKIE

>> A lot of times people don't like to raise their hand and ask a question in class. But actually, a lot of people think, "What did he mean?" It's really helpful to take advantage of office hours. I'll just go ask it, because I want to know! – STEPHANIE

Naixing worried that he would forget his questions or not know the words to explain himself in English. So before asking a teacher for help, he readied himself.

>> I always prepare a list of questions and practice them ahead of time. Then, after I get used to it, I go to find the teacher. One time, I was so nervous I couldn't speak. I just asked half the questions, and left the other half aside. – NAIXING

Debra, too, gained confidence by writing down her questions before she went to her professors.

>> It's refreshing to an instructor, in my experience, to have a student that cares about what they are there to learn. You show your professor that you are invested, instead of showing up one week before the end of the semester. If you get to a roadblock, you've got to ask for help. Don't be ashamed of it. How are you going to be smarter if you don't ask? So keep asking. – DEBRA

You might be surprised at how many of your teachers do care about your progress. Rena got a lot of support from professors who were committed to the education of Native American students.

>> I had so many people at the university that wanted to help me, that wanted me to succeed, and through my success they had some personal success. That's how it works. – RENA

If you have to miss a class, email the professor.

If you must miss a class, your professors will expect you to let them know in advance, either in person or by email. Tell the truth about why you could not come to class and, if necessary, ask how you can make up work.

Professors consider the way that you communicate with them a sign of your respect. If you take the same casual tone that you would in an instant message or an email to a friend, they react quite negatively. They are much more likely to take an interest in you if your email messages have a more professional tone, using correct English, spelling, and grammar. For example:

Dear Professor Cervone,

I'm writing to let you know that I have to miss class next Thursday due to a surgery I have had scheduled for several months in advance. I've tried to reschedule but was not able to. I will be sure to get the notes from a classmate. Thank you for understanding, and I'll see you on Thursday in two weeks. — *Abe Young*

When you've done well in a class, ask the professor for a recommendation.

If you have done well in a class, do not hesitate to ask the teacher to write you a general letter of recommendation for the file kept by your college's career services office. Later, when you are applying for graduate school or employment, that office will supply them to the right place upon request. The very best time to ask for a recommendation is right after a course ends, when the professor will best remember your strong points.

When you let them know you care about their field, professors also take a special interest in how you are doing later. After John Berry decided he wanted to major in history and later go on to graduate school, he made every effort to get to know the professors in that department on a friendly basis. He knew that if he did, their future recommendations would hold more meaning and insight.

>> I set up appointments with the faculty in that department to get to know them. I talked to my professors before and after class. They are people too, just like you! And college is about meeting people that can help you in the future. - JOHN

It's all right to remind a professor if you have requested a recommendation and it has not been sent. Most important, write a personal note of thanks after a professor has taken the time to supply one.

Ask other students for help.

Many first-generation college students notice that their classmates are much better prepared for demanding college work than they are. As you make connections with other students in and out of class, you can also call on them for help, feedback, and advice.

>> I needed to learn how to organize myself, to manage my time better and to improve my study skills. I got phone numbers of people I met in classes, and I would call and talk to them: "Oh, how do you do this, how do you study?" Then I would try different things until I found what was best for me. At first it was a struggle, but then I started getting the hang of it. - JACKIE

>> Some students have the advantage—they went to private schools and they know how to write good papers. So I got in the habit of emailing people my papers, like, "Would you read over this and make sure that it sounds parallel, that everything is formed the way it should be?" - ERIC

At first, John says, his pride kept him from asking other students for help. But he was holding down a part-time job, and he often could not get to the professor's office hours. To go after his education, he had to take the initiative.

>> It was just a matter of getting help when I needed help—not saying, "Oh, I can do this on my own." Math is probably my weakest subject, so I had to find somebody in my class that I knew was grasping the concepts, and would be willing to come in at six or seven at night and help me out. - JOHN

Debra has taken the lead in organizing students in her classes to get together and study.

>> The first day of classes, I pass around my notebook and ask my classmates for their name, phone number, and email. And if I get to a place where I'm not sure, I'll send out a mass email before a big test and ask, "Does anyone want to get together a study group?" You'd be surprised how many other students are feeling the same way, and welcome the chance to get together to study. - DEBRA

Take advantage of alumni networks.

You can also make important relationships with people who graduated from your college and are now making their way in the world. If you are seeking career advice, for example, or if you move to an unfamiliar city after graduating, alumni will often be ready to help, even if it has been many years since they graduated.

>> I'm going to L.A., I don't know anybody in L.A.—go to the alumni center and there's somebody from Northwestern in L.A., let me call them! That's how networking happens. Your college name has to do with everything, because they've been to the same school as you! There's tradition you can build off—maybe they've even had some of the same professors. – NIEMA

The career services office or the alumni relations office can help you find out the right alumni to contact for the particular need you might have. And once you graduate, you can join an email group that keeps you connected with others who graduated around the same time.

College is all about the people.

Even though your classes will teach you so much, the learning you do in college will often not take place in class. It will happen in your human encounters with people—whether they are other students, professors, administrators, advisers, or alumni. Every time you reach out to someone—to ask a question, to explore an idea, to explain something, to offer advice—you are deepening your college education.

For Rena, those interactions have given her "tools on how to live and ways to look at the world" that fit right in with her beliefs and values.

>> Education really alters you—you have all of these opportunities and experiences to look at the world in new ways and see things through other people's eyes. The best we can do as human beings is in sharing what we know, our knowledge of the world and experiences, just teaching one another, always reaching towards enlightenment of something, learning something you didn't know yesterday or ten minutes ago, and having a rich human interaction through experiences with other people. The idea that we are really all here to help each other, that's what guides me. – RENA

BUILDING MY NETWORK

Wherever you go in college, you will meet and get to know people who will be important in your life. These relationships will grow and build into a network that supports you personally and professionally. You can copy this worksheet to keep a record of their names, how you met, what you have in common, and any questions you might want to follow up on.

Name	
Where/how we met	
What we had in common	
Field of work	
Address	
Phone	
Email or website	
Notes	

Name	
Where/how we met	
What we had in common	
Field of work	
Address	
Phone	
Email or website	
Notes	

PROFESSORS TO STAY IN TOUCH WITH

Even after you finish a course, stay in contact with any professor you had a good connection with. Later, they might help you with your post-college planning (such as internships, graduate school, or work opportunities). You may also need to ask them for written recommendations in the future. Use this worksheet to keep track of their names and contact information, and add to your list every term.

TIP In the "Notes" column, write down anything you particularly liked or remember about this professor or course—a paper you wrote, a discussion you had, and so on. This helps you reconnect with the professor if time goes by before you are in contact again.

Term and year	
Professor's name	
Course you took	
Professor's email	
Phone	
Notes	

Term and year	
Professor's name	
Course you took	
Professor's email	
Phone	
Notes	

Term and year	
Professor's name	
Course you took	
Professor's email	
Phone	
Notes	

Term and year	
Professor's name	
Course you took	
Professor's email	
Phone	
Notes	

Term and year	
Professor's name	
Course you took	
Professor's email	
Phone	
Notes	

5

The Hours of Your Day

How to manage your time and resources

*D*uring her first year at college, Stephanie Serda lived at home with her mother, her two younger brothers, and their grandfather, a short drive from the Ohio state university she attends. It was a tough year. Her parents were in the middle of a divorce, and Stephanie felt the stress of staying loyal to both of them, while also helping her younger brothers deal with their feelings. She worked a part-time job to earn spending money, but she also worried about keeping up with her studies in the middle of her large extended family.

>> I had my own room, and I would close my door a lot. During the week, when it was just the family there, it was like, "She's in college, you have to be quiet." But on the weekends, I still have to study. And since my grandpa lives with my mom, a lot of my aunts and uncles and cousins come over a lot, so you can't get work done. – STEPHANIE

Stephanie's strategies paid off, and she finished her first year with very good grades. But by living at home, she felt that she was missing out on the college social scene. For her sophomore year, she moved into a dorm on campus, and right away she found herself swept up in new friendships and activities.

>> That semester I got the worst grades in my whole history at school. I skipped classes too, like, "Oh, I need to sleep in." I joined more groups, and I didn't manage my time as well as far as studying. And I barely read at all. – STEPHANIE

For her third year, Stephanie moved into an apartment near the campus, sharing it with a cousin. She paid her rent and food expenses with money saved from her summer job, but she soon found herself running low. Rather than taking a job that would cut back on her time to study, she decided to move back home, this time to her father's house.

>> I didn't want to have to stress about paying the bills and getting good grades all at the same time. I knew that it would be quieter at my dad's, so I could get more schoolwork done. And also he doesn't live in my old neighborhood, where I would be distracted by a lot of other things. – STEPHANIE

Many other first-generation college students face the problem Stephanie was dealing with: emotional, financial, physical, academic, and time stresses, all at once. If you try to ignore them, these strains can wear you out. Addressing them step by step, as Stephanie did, will make a huge difference to how well you do in college.

Plan for a living situation that will best support your studies.

College students often decide where to live based on the cost to them. But as you calculate that cost, remember that it will cost you, in the long run, if your lifestyle does not support your study habits. Whether you live in a dorm, rent an off-campus apartment, or stay at home, plan carefully for quiet time and space for your academic work.

When she lived at her mother's house, for example, Stephanie often did her homework on campus to get away from the bustle of home.

>> I would come to the library a lot—both the town library and the one on campus. There's also a tech lab on campus that's open 24 hours; I could just go there and work on a paper or something for a while. – STEPHANIE

When he needs a computer, Naixing also used the ones at City College of San Francisco, because he did not have one at his parents' home.

>> At home I have a study place, my bedroom. I stay there to do my homework, just using pencil and paper. – NAIXING

Jackie commuted to her college classes in Denver from her mother's house. Family and friends often got together at their home, and if she had homework to do, she had to speak up directly.

>> My mom's boyfriend lived there as well, and my uncle was staying in our living room for a while, because he was going through a hard time. I had

my own room, but I didn't have a desk, so I usually just studied at the kitchen table. There were a lot of people in and out—sometimes they brought their friends and partied, and played cards, and it did get hard. I told them, "I'm not trying to be rude, but if I want to do good in school I need some peace and quiet." And they looked at me like, "I don't understand why you have to be that way." - JACKIE

Sharing space with other students—in a dormitory, a fraternity or sorority, or an apartment—you may have many of the same issues.

》 You learn how to deal with people, you learn how to communicate when you have a very small space to share with somebody. And if you happen to have somebody that's completely opposite from you, it's a living hell. Colleges usually don't do a good job matching you with the right person, and you have to sacrifice a lot, if you're very picky about your personal space. - MALY

If other students have created a party atmosphere that makes it hard to study, it can feel uncomfortable to say so. Maly's freshman-year roommate used their room as a gathering place, which led to problems they ultimately resolved.

》 We were listening to different types of music, she was very outgoing, and she was already a step ahead of me. I was still trying to make the room my little sacred place, and she was making it her party place! So we definitely had a clash in there. We tried to deal with that, we tried to communicate, we tried to work things out—sometimes it works, sometimes it doesn't. For us, it was better to stay friends but live separately. So I moved to a different room. - MALY

Having to commute a long distance to college also puts a strain on your time and resources. Karen Priest decided to enroll at Oklahoma State, more than half an hour's drive from where she lived with her husband and her young son. Because she could not drive, she thought about moving the whole family to be near the college, but her husband needed to stay close to his sick father. So Karen looked for a place to live with her son near the campus, going back home on weekends.

>> This is my personality: I was willing to live in a tent and ride a bicycle to class, take showers at the Wellness Center. But I found out that they had married-student housing up here, and my scholarships cover that—so I didn't have to live in a tent. – KAREN

Pay attention to your body clock, and find ways to deal with it.

Like many people of college age, Hazel is not a morning person. She really liked her college classes, but if she wanted to do well in them, she had to reset her body clock.

>> There are days when I just want to lay in bed all day, and just say, "Screw class." But you know, it's just a matter of accepting your responsibility. I wanted to go to school in the first place, I wanted to sign up for these classes, so I might as well take advantage of them. – HAZEL

In the end, she decided to go out less in the evenings, so she could get to bed earlier.

>> I have a really, really busy lifestyle, and it took me a while to get in the habit of getting up early, and getting to class by nine. But I do it. I just have to force myself to go to bed really early—which is hard, because there's great stuff to do at night. – HAZEL

Naixing, too, tries to remember how he feels the next day in class if he doesn't get enough sleep.

>> If I was studying or watching TV too late, or I went to hang out with friends and went to bed late, then in the morning I feel really sleepy and I don't want to go to school. But when I think about how important it is, and my grades and that kind of stuff, I encourage myself to go to school no matter what. – NAIXING

Make a plan for how to use the time available to you.

When Debra began again at the Community College of Denver, at the age of 26, she already had several young boys at home. To manage the competing demands of academics and parenting, she looked hard at her schedule.

>> You have your schedule in front of you; you know how many classes you are taking. With the time that's not scheduled for classes, budget time for studying. When a friend asks you to do something, say, "Sure, I'd like to go to that movie with you, but I'm scheduled to study from six to nine tonight." – DEBRA

As a high school athlete, Stephen had a busy schedule of school and sports. At the University of Texas, he had much more freedom, but his commitments multiplied. He realized he had to develop new skills to balance his time.

>> In college, I'm a very different kind of busy. And you don't have someone there holding your hand, making sure that your schedule's laid out. I went to sleep at seven this morning, and the night before, I went to sleep at six. – STEPHEN

With a full course load at his university in Fort Wayne, a work-study job on campus, and a night-shift restaurant job on weekends, John decided to write down his complicated schedule and check it every day.

>> It's just a matter of really scheduling things. I use one planner for my life and a separate planner for my homework assignments. I write out my schedule and check my syllabus every day to make sure there are no surprises. Keeping up with the syllabus, that's the biggest thing. I always have time built into the day to do my homework. I've got it down: "Okay, it's three o'clock on a Wednesday, I'm done with class, I don't have to work till five. I have two hours, this is what I have to do for the next day." I don't work nights on the days I have class, just on the weekends. I have Sundays off, so I can get sleep, do laundry, clean house, whatever I need to do. – JOHN

Aileen was used to balancing a part-time job with her school and family responsibilities. But when she got to college, her classes became more demanding, and her family still had three young children running around. Knowing how high the stakes were, Aileen made strict rules about when she would do her homework.

>> I always give myself enough time to give it in on time. I just stay after work two or three extra hours to do my schoolwork. Or when I get out of work, I go to the library and finish. I only use the computer at home late at night, when everybody's sleeping, if I have to do some research or type something real quick. Sometimes I have to stay up late to study, but I don't stay up all night, 'cause then I'll fall asleep in class. – AILEEN

Extracurricular activities are an important part of college, but they also take up a lot of time. In her first year at Northwestern, Niema joined the campus chapter of the National Association of Black Journalists, and when elections came she ran for secretary. Right away, she realized she would have to adjust her other commitments.

>> I thought: Okay, if I am going to run I need to write my speech, and that has to sideline a lot of things that are going on right now. But if I win, the position is for the whole school year. How would being on this board affect what I'm able to do next year as a sophomore? Those are the type of questions that you have to answer for yourself. – NIEMA

At her state university in Ohio, Stephanie had to balance her studies with her involvement in the Latino Students Union (LSU). She also wanted to play competitive intramural sports, so she divided her activities across the academic year.

>> During the first semester, I played coed football and basketball, and that was all I did. I didn't play second semester, so I had more time. I went to LSU meetings once a week, to plan social events and stuff like that. – STEPHANIE

Keep track of college deadlines for choosing classes.

When you have to balance your time so carefully in order to do well, choosing the right courses becomes even more important. This is particularly important for students who need extra support academically. At a big college or university, courses fill up quickly, and unless you stay very organized you may miss your chance to enroll in the ones you want.

Aside from fulfilling the requirements for his major, Naixing was always looking for three key things when he signed up for courses: an interesting teacher, a subject he cared about, and a class where he was not the only one to need extra help. He learned to register online as early as possible, then move quickly to change his decisions if he saw that a class was not right for him.

>> For online registration, they tell you the date and the time you can register —for instance, February 22, one o'clock. So on that day, go online at one o'clock to get into the good spots. On the first day of class, if you don't like the class, you can decide to change to another. But don't wait too late—you have to find another class instantly, otherwise you will miss your spot.
— NAIXING

Take action right away if you start to fall behind.

At times, personal problems such as sickness or family troubles may cause you to fall behind in your studies. John's grandmother fell ill, and he missed a week of class when he went home to help. He worried most about catching up in math, which was one of his most challenging subjects.

>> In a math class, you always build on the last concept you learned. And college level courses are so much faster—you learn a concept every week. If you can't make it to class for a week, you're behind, and by the time you figure it out, you're behind two weeks! - JOHN

When he got back to school from the time with his family, he went right to the professor and explained his situation.

>> It just takes saying, "All right, this is why I'm behind," whether it's a good reason or not. If it's a bad reason, like "I was tired," hopefully you don't do it again. But if you have a death in the family or something, there's ways that the class can be extended, they maybe give you an extra couple of weeks. Worst case, you can take an incomplete for that class and maybe retake it next semester. - JOHN

John had to catch up in all his classes, but he used one strategy for math class and another in courses where he had fallen behind in the reading.

>> If I get behind in a reading-intensive course, I start from where they're at in the class, and when I get time later, I pick up the stuff I missed. In math, I spend more time getting myself up to speed—with tutoring, and talking to the professor after class—rather than just saying, "The heck with it." Don't do that! If you actively seek out to get caught up, little by little you will. – JOHN

When she moved from home into a college dormitory for her second year, Stephanie began to enjoy a more active social life, and her grades dropped. Right away, she decided to do something about it.

>> I got two Ds and some Cs, and I knew I could have gotten a lot better. I retook the D classes, even though I didn't have to, because I didn't want them to be on my grade point average. And the next semester, spring of last year, I actually made the dean's list. – STEPHANIE

Limit your workload to what you know you can handle.

You will need practical ways to manage the stresses that come when time, money, and course work conflict with each other. After dropping out of high school because she was bored, Hazel spent a couple of years working at low-paying jobs with no future. When she finally went back, she enrolled in a special program where she could earn her high school diploma while also taking courses for college credit. It took a lot of effort to balance everything on her plate, but she had made up her mind to do it.

>> There's tricks that you have to learn to not dropping out. I'm a triple threat: I have high school, college, and a job. So I make sure that I'll have time to do everything I need to do, without killing myself. If I have to take just one college class per semester to make it work, I will. But if I know a little bit about this and that subject, and I'm pretty sure I can handle two college classes in a semester, then I'll do it. You always gotta make sure that you have a work load that you can carry, or else you'll just quit. You have to learn when to take a break, or else you'll just hate it. And you will burn out so fast. – HAZEL

Raja decided to work more than thirty hours a week to help pay for his college. He scheduled all his classes on three days, and used the other days to work in a local market. But he doesn't recommend it.

>> You'll find yourself not having time for anything else. When you don't have time to see friends, or go to the rec center, or do any activity other than school or work, you eventually get frustrated with the whole thing. And that gets your motivation down, and you don't want to do as well, or you find short cuts and you stop going to class just to rest. If you're going to have to miss class to go to work, I suggest not even working, and just dealing with that for now, and getting a loan or something. Because you won't learn anything that way. – RAJA

Put your education before your paying job.

As Raja discovered, financial pressures can easily threaten your college studies. If that happens to you, look for every possible way to cut back on your paying job. It's not easy to set that priority, as Jackie also found. While in college, she lived first with her mother and then with her father, contributing to the household expenses.

>> When one of my parents would get laid off and couldn't afford to support me, that made it even harder to stay in school. There was one point where I was working at a work-study job and my dad was unemployed and I had to find a way to pay as much bills as I could, plus trying to pitch in for some food, and I was going to school full time. It makes me think I just want to get a full-time job and live on my own, so my parents won't have to worry about how they're going to feed me. – JACKIE

Despite her worries, however, Jackie kept going in school. She didn't want to stop the momentum she had built up toward a career that would bring her both satisfaction and more money.

>> My mom didn't understand why I couldn't go to college and have a job. She wanted me to help out, and to her it didn't seem that hard, because she didn't really know what college entailed. I felt bad about it, but I had to explain, "Mom, this is hard for me, and I can't do it." I finally just got a work-study job, two hours a day. – JACKIE

As an older student who had spent years in the work force before starting college, John wanted to pack as much paying work as possible into his week. But he knew he should not cut back on his classes—in part, because full-time students qualify for more financial aid. In the end, John also decided that it made more sense to make academics his top priority.

» Figure out how much you need to make, and work a paying job as little as you have to. If you just need to pay for your car insurance and go out on the weekend, there's no need to be working 40 hours, and you might say, "Fifteen hours is all I'm going to work for pay." But that's not an option if you have a family, where you have to pay your house payment, feed your kids, things like that. – JOHN

When he started to feel overwhelmed by the reading and writing required of him, John learned to take a hard look at his course selections.

» Maybe you shouldn't take three reading-intensive courses in one semester. Maybe instead you should take this class that you were planning on taking next year, because it's a little less work. – JOHN

If class work spikes during one semester, you might also talk to your employer about reducing your work hours temporarily. Jackie found that when she took two tough science classes in one semester, she had to cut back on her work-study hours.

» Even this semester, I'm still learning my balance in college. My work-study is letting me do fifteen hours a week, and that may be just a little bit too much, for as hard classes as I have. So I talked to my work-study boss, and we both decided that we're going to cut down my hours and I'm going to catch up on my reading. Time is more precious than money. – JACKIE

Remember that federal student aid will often help pay for your living expenses, freeing up more time to study. Naixing held down a part-time job when he started at the City College of San Francisco, but his grades were not as high as he hoped. With the help of student aid, he increased his course load and put all his energy into his schoolwork.

» Since I am taking 17 units, I really wanted to focus my studies and hopefully I can do better, compared to last semester. – NAIXING

Make a plan for how to use the money available to you.

Like many first-generation college students, Eric Polk found it hard to have a lot less money than most of his classmates. He tried not to spend it on things that wouldn't help him get to graduation.

» Situations where other people have money and I don't–I still deal with that, emotionally. If three or four of my friends were going out and I didn't have the cash to go, I wouldn't go. I have my priorities first. Right now, I still don't have one of my books for one of my classes. If going out and having a good time is going to mess up a chance for me to do better in my class and get a credit that I need, then I'm going to keep my ten dollars and put it toward that book. – ERIC

Jackie lived with one or the other of her parents, helping with the food and utility bills when she could. She didn't ask them for money, but she sometimes used the money she earned to boost her morale with a treat for herself.

» I've had a work-study job, to pay some of my bills and also maybe go to a weekend movie or buy some nice clothes here and there. I try to explain to my mom, that's my reward to myself for working so hard. Now that I've become a woman, I need to have decent clothes instead of rags, you know? – JACKIE

Aileen lived at home, too, but she had a part-time job as well as going to school. She paid her own expenses, then contributed to the family from what was left over.

» My mother and me and my sister, we all help each other. I use my paycheck to pay my car insurance, my cell phone, my clothes, everything for myself. And I help my mother with whatever I can, like the clothes for my three nephews that live with us. – AILEEN

Because John worked full time before he went to college, he found it hard to adapt his life to a reduced income.

>> They say you should only work twenty hours a week, but if I work twenty hours a week, I'm on the street. I get grants and loans, so my tuition and books, they're paid for. But I still had my car payment and my rent to pay, phone bill, electric bill, groceries... I did an itemized budget of how much I needed to make, and then I went to look for a job that would match up to that. – JOHN

He juggled his paycheck with college financial aid, and by his third year of college he had figured out how to balance his budget.

>> I'm taking out more loans now, and getting grants that I didn't get at first. We get our financial aid checks at the end of August and the middle of January, so I use those to pay off my rent. Then my biweekly paycheck pays for my gas, and my financial aid covers my books. – JOHN

Students in this book emphasized two major strategies that helped them stay out of financial trouble:

Buying used books. John saves a lot of money by buying almost all of his books used, on the Internet..

>> With a little research you can find web sites like half.com and ecampus.com, where used textbooks sell really cheap. They might be marked in a little bit, but there's not pages missing or anything. I go to the bookstore to get the ISBN numbers off the books, and then look them up on the Internet. It's easier just to put the ISBN number into your search engine, because it will go right to the edition that you need, and there's a new edition every two years. At the bookstore it might cost 80, 90 dollars for a used textbook, and I'll find it on the Internet for 20 bucks. – JOHN

Keeping credit card use to a bare minimum. Karen has seen many first-generation students sink into financial trouble as they take the credit card offers that come in the mail. Unless they pay off their card in full every month, their debts quickly pile up.

>> You really don't know the implications if you overextend on your credit. When you use the card, you're going to have to make a payment within a month, and you have to come up with that money somehow. Especially

if you're not working, a lot of students do get in that bind. If it's your first time away from home, it's open field for anything. – KAREN

As you approach graduation, banks may flood you with tempting offers of credit cards with limits high enough to pay off your student loans. Use extreme caution! If you miss even one payment on a credit card, your rate can skyrocket. Your federal student loans will give you better protection. (You can download excellent advice for students on credit card use at www.studentaid.org.)

Take advantage of college resources that can help you.

Your college wants you to succeed, and it provides many different ways to help with the different problems you encounter. Finding the right place to live, understanding your financial aid paperwork, dealing with transportation problems—all these issues can work out more quickly if you find the right office on campus to ask.

» At Northwest Indian College, it's such a community and everybody there is working for the success of the students. I had an adviser who was especially key. She gave a class on how to fill out the financial aid forms and scholarship applications, which I still use. Once you get the key things down, there's so much money out there to be had. Just keep trying, keep applying. If you don't get one, just go on to the next application and try again. – RENA

In Denver, both Debra and Jackie found support through a special program for first-generation students.

» It definitely helped me acclimate to the college environment. Being a first-generation student means that you are in unfound territory, there's no one who's gone before you, that you are close to, that can tell you all the ins and outs, give you all the ups and downs. You are on your own; you're going to have to learn on your own. First Generation taught me how to apply for my courses, what courses I would need, what would come in the following semester, how credits apply—all the things a student needs to know. – DEBRA

Later, Jackie got a work-study job in the same office. Now, she is the one to help other students.

>> I'm a student ambassador there, so I have a caseload of students to keep track of. I contact them twice a week, about different things—deadlines, help with financial aid, how are they doing in class, do they need a tutor or a counselor? - JACKIE

At Oklahoma State, Karen checked out of her student apartment when she left campus for the summer term. Returning early with her young son from their time away, she had trouble getting back into their place. She turned for help to the college adviser for Native American students.

>> He made some phone calls to the housing office, and sure enough, I got in the next day. Later, I had another friend who thought his gas and electric was going to get cut off, and the same adviser found out there was money available to help. - KAREN

Debra knocked on door after door at her college in Denver to get the answers she needed.

>> How you're going to pay for college, how you're going to support yourself, how you are going to pick your classes, how you are going to register, the books—ask someone to explain it to you. And if you don't understand what they tell you, ask someone else. If you don't know why your award letter has something written on it, don't just say, "It will come to me later." Go find out. - DEBRA

In some cases, she had to do a little research to know the right question to ask, before she found someone for help.

>> Sometimes looking on the Internet can help you figure out the questions to go ask someone in person. Take the initiative. Then you are in charge of your own future. - DEBRA

Once they got control over the basics of time and money, students like Debra could better handle the next challenge—doing well in their academics. In the next chapter, they will tell how they took the initiative in that area, too.

MY WEEKLY CLASS SCHEDULE

As you choose your courses, write the times they meet into this schedule. This will help you avoid time conflicts and organize your day into classes, study time, work, and other activities. (You can copy the blank form and keep using it throughout your time at college.)

Term _____ Year _____

Time period	Monday	Tuesday	Wednesday	Thursday	Friday	Saturday

HOW DO I USE MY TIME?

You will need to think carefully about how you balance your time among different things: classes, studying and homework, working at your job, eating, sleeping, clubs or activities, exercise, and so forth. Especially in your first few weeks at college, you might wonder where all the time goes. Even though it may seem crazy, writing down what you do for a whole week can help you figure that out. Photocopy the grid on the next page (using the largest paper size available) and fill it in once a day. At the end of the week, analyze the grid to find areas that compete with each other, taking notes in the space below. You can then adjust your daily habits to make the very best use of your time.

Notes, ideas, reflections: _____

_____

_____

_____

_____

_____

_____

_____

_____

_____

_____

_____

_____

_____

_____

_____

Time	Mon	Tues	Wed	Thurs	Fri	Sat	Sun
6 a.m.							
7 a.m.							
8 a.m.							
9 a.m.							
10 a.m.							
11 a.m.							
12 p.m.							
1 p.m.							
2 p.m.							
3 p.m.							
4 p.m.							
5 p.m.							
6 p.m.							
7 p.m.							
8 p.m.							
9 p.m.							
10 p.m.							
11 p.m.							
12 a.m.							
1 a.m.							
2 a.m.							
3 a.m.							
4 a.m.							
5 a.m.							

6

Reading, Writing, and Aiming High

Your critical college skills can only get better

When she enrolled in the Community College of Denver at the age of 26, Debra Graves had already faced enough trouble for a lifetime. Without a stable parent in her life, in sixth grade she quit school and left home, and by fourteen Debra had a child herself. While living in a battered women's shelter, she earned her high school equivalency degree at seventeen. But her first try at college did not go well, and she flunked out.

By the time she tried again, Debra had decided to build her own family's future on the foundation of her college education. "Education has changed my life," she says about the past three years. "It is the one thing I can do at my own pace and that I can be really good at." She has four sons now, and they inspire her to keep on going for a university degree after she finishes with community college.

For Debra, doing college right meant having the courage to go back to square one. She saw the college's academic support system of her as a lifeline, and she used it to strengthen her skills and move forward on her own.

>> If I want to get an A on a paper, I know what that means. It means I work harder on that paper, I do better research, I find papers others students wrote years ago and see how they did theirs. Nobody can prevent me, no one can stop me from doing well. I can be my own master. - DEBRA

Debra has had to work hard to earn her grades, and she feels great satisfaction in that. At home, she is passing along to her boys the methods she learned in college.

>> My boys are required to do math facts and reading every night. And when they want something, I tell them to write me an essay, I want it edited, proofed, revised, typed up and brought to me. They are very clear in my expectations in that area. - DEBRA

Debra's story shows the importance of starting where you are academically, and also of aiming high. In this chapter, she and other students describe how they got from square one to their college diploma, step by step.

Find out what resources your college provides for academic help.

If you are stuck on how to organize a paper or solve a math problem, your college has places you can turn for help. At tutoring and resource centers—and sometimes right in your dormitory—advanced students or special staff members will coach you on writing, math, or other academic issues you have.

» Don't be ashamed to go to a tutor. In high school, I thought I was supposed to know everything, but when I got here, it was like, "I need some help!" – ERIC

When you have trouble in any particular class, you should ask the professor if tutoring can be arranged. Most likely, you will be paired with a student who is paid by the college to help you.

» The student tutors at the writing center had a background in English, and you could tell they knew what they were talking about. They worked with you, they took their time with you, and that's how I really did good with English and got my skills up for writing research papers. Now I have this real good tutor for biology, and I'm trying to get her for chemistry, too. She is a student but she happens to be a really good teacher as well. – JACKIE

Manage your reading load.

Even students who come from very demanding high schools often feel shocked at how much reading most college courses require. In reality, one fact of life about college is that almost nobody can actually do all of the assigned reading in all their classes. Yet developing ways to manage it is worth the trouble it takes. The skills of reading and understanding materials in a time-effective way will benefit you not just throughout college, but all your life long.

If you are not used to reading so much difficult material, or if you have limited English, you will need a plan to deal with several issues:

- What is most important to read, and what you can safely skip

- How to skim a text while still understanding the material

- How to remember what you read

- How to use what you read to do well in class and on papers

- How to select your courses so that you balance your reading load

As a history major, John found himself overwhelmed by his reading requirements.

》 In my freshman history class, we had a textbook and three novels to read. The novels were about 250 pages apiece, and in sixteen weeks you have to keep up on your textbook reading, plus class lectures, plus these three novels, and then you have to write papers on these three novels. So you're going through a new novel about every three weeks. – JOHN

He quickly decided to spend minimal time on reading the textbook, using it only for reference.

》 Textbooks you don't read word for word. You just get the main ideas out of it, along with what's discussed in class, and you have a pretty good grasp. A lot of my upper-level classes don't even use textbooks. We use primary source documents that the professor puts together in a nice little book, and you read a couple of articles per class period. – JOHN

Milenny, too, had a rude shock in her first year at Wheaton College, when she saw how much reading her professors assigned.

》 I was really upset because no matter how hard I tried, I wasn't doing enough. The only way I saw to do better was to just bury myself in the library and never leave. Before, I thought that if they assigned fifteen chapters or something, I had to read every word, every page, every single little thing. And then after a while once you get the rhythm of the professor and what you actually need to learn, it wasn't as hard any more, and I just learned how to pick out the important facts. – MILENNY

Effective reading and note-taking skills do not come naturally to most people. Yet they make all the difference when it comes time to study for exams, write research papers, make presentations, and participate in class discussions. And they also save you time! Signing up for help with reading skills at your college's academic resource center will put you a giant step ahead in many of the courses you take. (See page 117 for one suggestion on a reading method that can help.)

Writing is everything.

Just as with reading, learning to write well is not easy. Writing is thinking on paper—and the more you practice writing clearly, the more clearly you will find yourself thinking. As a first-generation student, learning to write will pay off more than any other skill that you develop in your college years. In a very real way, it is what you are at college for, because it can put you on an equal footing with others who have a head start.

Writing will help you succeed in college—when you write papers, when you apply for a class that you really want to take or a position on a committee you care about, when you write letters applying for financial support. As you apply for internships and jobs, whatever the field, good writing skills will help you stand out. Even in your private life, writing can help you say what you really mean when it matters most.

In fact, writing is such a personal act of connection that sometimes it can expose your deepest self. When she turned in her first college paper, Debra felt on top of the world. Then came the blow.

>> In front of the entire class the instructor handed me my paper and said, "Debra, you need to go to the writing lab to learn how to write more college-level material." I was devastated, I was so crushed. I looked at the grade, it was a C minus, and I said, " Oh, God, my life is over." I was so humiliated: "What made me think I could do this?" I don't think I heard anything else the instructor said in the class that day. I went straight home, ran into the bathroom and started crying. – DEBRA

After she dried her eyes, Debra picked herself up and took herself to the college writing lab.

>> I ended up getting an A on the next assignment and every assignment after that, and I finished that semester on the vice-president's list. If I had quit,

I never would have known what I was capable of. Sure, it was embarrassing to have people dissect my work and put it all back together. It was really tough. But it made me so much better for that. I learned how to write college-level material. Better yet, I got published in my third semester. – DEBRA

When she started taking college classes, Hazel had never written a long paper before. In order to focus and organize her thoughts for more than a few pages, she had to ask someone for help.

» I knew how to write short papers from high school, but I didn't know how to write a twelve-page paper without rambling. How do I make it sound like I'm not crazy? I didn't want to ask the teacher for help, because I thought it would make me look weaker than the other students. But you're going to feel so stupid when you've worked on this thing so hard, and just because you didn't ask the right questions, you don't end up getting a good grade.
HAZEL

John, too, started college without the basic writing skills he needed. During his first year, he took two remedial writing courses in a row, and he also used peer editors at the college's writing center.

» My writing teacher got to the point: "You can do better than this." She's like, "I can see you have good ideas, you just don't know how to put them together." So I would write my first draft and take it in to the writing center. A half hour to an hour later, you have all these ideas how to shorten it, expand it, grammar, and everything. – JOHN

John realized that the most important thing was getting something down on paper to begin with. He sought out any reader who would give him feedback. Then he revised again and again.

» You give it your best shot, get those ideas out of your head, print it off and look over it—and you turn in the draft to your professor. Then you have to take it back, learn what they're looking for in this paper, make those corrections. If you're still not happy with it or not sure what they want, take that second draft back to them, too. Say, "Can you look over this?" If they can't, find somebody that can. Somewhere in your university, somebody knows how to write that paper. – JOHN

As he paid attention to what worked and what didn't, John developed confidence as a writer and started to do well on his college papers.

>> I never had the greatest education when I was growing up. To this day, I still can't spell very well, and my grammar is horrible. But what I have been able to develop is, I know how to write a paper: Okay, these are the sources I have, this is how you put all the sources together. A lot of it is learning the styles of writing. Then it's practice, practice, practice, practice. More practice. – JOHN

For Rena, studying writing in college also opened a whole world of personal expression, giving voice to her powerful imagination and ideas. Right after receiving her college diploma, she went East to study for a masters degree in poetry. Someday, she will take what she learns back home.

>> As soon as I have my M.F.A., I want to teach English writing and Native American literature at our tribal college. – RENA

Recognize and take pride in your own accomplishments.

As you develop your reading and writing skills, you will probably start to do better in all your college classes. But time after time, you will also have to pick yourself up from disappointment. It's very important to give yourself the credit you deserve for simply trying hard and keeping on going.

Jackie had a hard time in her first college biology class, but she knew she would have to do well in that subject to follow her chosen path in dentistry. She kept working hard in the next level class, and the concepts started to take hold in her mind. This time, she earned top grades—and her confidence went up, too.

>> I may have not had biology in high school—so guess what: I'll struggle the first semester. But the second semester and the third, I'll get better and better. I studied very hard the first term, but I ended up getting a C, and that's good for that class! And I just aced the next course. – JACKIE

John repeated one of his college math classes because he did not grasp the concepts the first time around. He refused to get discouraged because he did not get top grades in a subject where he lacked a solid background.

>> I got Cs in all my math classes, thank God! Am I happy with those Cs? No, because I have a higher level of expectation for myself. But are those realistic grades for me? Yes, I believe that is the best I could have done. I came from a person who barely knew algebra to passing a class in trigonometry. You know, that was a major accomplishment for me. – JOHN

College is a long haul, and everyone gets their fair share of hard times. Like John, you can be realistic and positive at the same time. Don't forget to celebrate your successes, small and large.

>> The first test that I got back in my first college class, I got an A on! I was so excited, I went home and put it up with a little magnet frame on the refrigerator. When my parents walked in I was like, "Hey Mom! Look at the fridge! Check out my grade!" I was telling everybody: my aunt who lives in Chicago, my grandma. I felt so good that I put in the time to study and I got a good grade. All those times that my mom said, "If you work hard, good things will happen," she wasn't just lying! It's really true. – HAZEL

As she began to plan for her next degree after community college, Debra had a sense of pride and accomplishment. She had come a long way from her high school dropout days, and she was going even farther.

>> When I get an A, it's amazing, I know I did that, that it's my work and I'm the one who gets the credit and no one can stop me. Besides, I like the feeling of knowing stuff. When my boys ask me a question and I can answer it, they think I know everything! – DEBRA

WHAT DO I WANT FOR MYSELF?

You are more likely to achieve your academic and personal goals if you break them down into smaller parts. Use the first part of this worksheet to make notes on what academic skills you need for each class and how you can get help on them. In the second part of the worksheet, make notes about how you hope to develop in non-academic ways (for example, through activities that may enrich your life or reduce your stress).

In My Courses

Class: _____

_____

To do better in this class, what could I work on? _____

_____

_____

Who I can ask for help with this: _____

_____

_____

Class: _____

_____

To do better in this class, what could I work on? _____

_____

_____

Who I can ask for help with this: _____

_____

_____

In Other Areas

Category:_____
_____

To develop in this area, what do I need to do or learn? _____
_____
_____

Who or what might support me in this?_____
_____
_____

Category: _____
_____

To develop in this area, what do I need to do or learn? _____
_____
_____

Who or what might support me in this? _____
_____
_____

7

Good Times and Hard Times

Maly Fung comes from a close and traditional Chinese family. Her parents immigrated from a rural area of China to Venezuela, where Maly and her siblings grew up speaking both Chinese and Spanish. When time came for high school, the family picked up and moved again—this time to Queens, a borough of New York City. Maly's parents wanted their children to prepare for college in the United States, so she went to a city public school for immigrant students.

She had another culture shock when she accepted a scholarship to Lafayette College, a selective private college in the Lehigh Valley of Pennsylvania. About two hours' drive from her home, it felt like a different universe.

>> I'm a very metropolitan person, I like to walk around and go to different places. But when you're dorming at Lafayette, it's Friday night and what do you do? There's not that many options. The crickets are crying! And there's nothing going on but a house party or a frat party! – MALY

For her first weeks at college, Maly called home almost every night, weeping. But then she decided that she would never be happy unless she once again could accept and adjust to a new environment. She joined the international students association, and made good friends there. And she kept always in her mind the thought that her education mattered—not just for herself but for her family.

>> They are the reason why I am doing this. I want to be somebody for them, I want to be successful so they can be proud. But it's for me, too. I've come all this way... I want to feel I have achieved something. – MALY

Maly's positive attitude got her through, and four years later she graduated and came back to New York. She always felt like something of an

outsider at her college in the countryside. But she had also found things in common with classmates whose backgrounds were nothing like hers.

>> You definitely feel conflicted when you stand out in a group, and you're going through different experiences. You feel a little bit discouraged. But if you already stand out, you might as well shine. When you talk to people, you realize that they also go through problems. It's not that different from anybody else. – MALY

In this chapter, first-generation students describe their good times as well as their hard times as they got used to the social and emotional aspects of college life. Like them, you can make friendships that expand your world, help you learn, and also provide you with emotional support. And like them, you can also find other places to turn when college feels too overwhelming—including your counselors and advisers, your loved ones, and even yourself.

Find different ways to make friends.

When she first got to college, Jackie's homework crowded out her time to make new friends. Looking at the problem more closely, she decided that she would try to make friends by studying together.

>> I would talk to people in my class, a little at a time. I would ask them a question or crack a joke, and then I would get someone's phone number and say, "Let's study together," or something like that. – JACKIE

Karen, a Native American student in Oklahoma, reminded herself that cultural factors might be preventing students like her from making that first move.

>> A lot of Native students, they don't want to make a scene. The way I was raised, when you're quiet, it shows respect. You have to get out of that mindset, put your hand out there, open your mouth. You might have to take that first step. You know, the other student is just as scared as you are. But someone has to break that ice. – KAREN

Stephanie lived at home during her first year, which did save some money. But she looked wistfully at the new friendships made by her best friend from high school, who lived in a dorm.

>> So for my sophomore year, I actually moved to the dorms, and I made a lot of friends. I didn't think it would be all it was, and I was wrong. It's something that everyone should do for at least one year, because you meet a lot of people and it's a lot of fun. – STEPHANIE

Look for others who have something in common with you.

Karen came from a small community, and when she started at Oklahoma State University she felt overwhelmed by how huge and impersonal it felt.

>> I remember my first, second day on campus, I could not believe all these students! I had tears in my eyes, and I thought, What am I going to do?! And then I saw this one guy from Oklahoma City, and I was like, "Oh! Come here, I need a hug!" – KAREN

Seeking out other Native American students on campus also helped her find her balance.

>> I think it's important that we find our niche, find people like us. There's a special house where a lot of Native Americans live, and there's a Native students club that meets biweekly, we have pow-wows and take trips. There's also this program to help minority students transition. – KAREN

As a Chinese immigrant who was still learning English, Naixing felt shy when he started community college in San Francisco. He started by making friends with students who spoke his language. But then he gathered his courage to start conversations with others who had interests in common with him.

>> I saw someone doing math homework, and I asked him, "Are you taking calculus?" I told him that I took it already, and if you need help, you can go to the library. So I was giving a lot of suggestions to him, and then we started to make friends. We say hello to each other on campus, and whenever we are coming on the bus we sit together and have a conversation.

For me, ethnicity or race is not really a barrier. If someone has the same interests as yours, you will make friends. – NAIXING

Maly joined a feminist student group and another group that worked for social justice. She appreciated the close friends she made, but she also felt that she was making a difference in an area that mattered to her.

>> In a way it's kind of a small community within the college community. You meet people that have the same mentality, the same aspirations that you do. It reinforces your will to fight for those causes. That's something that I really like about college, you find people that are like-minded. – MALY

People you meet in student organizations can expand your world.

As he participated in various student clubs and organizations, Stephen also found himself building a network of new friends, and their activities together had much to teach him.

>> I got involved in the intergroup dialogue class, with the Latino students. The theory behind it is you take groups of people who wouldn't normally sit down at the table and discuss the issues that affect their relationships, in society or interpersonally. We talked about race, religion, ageism, gender, sexism... Those are things that aren't discussed a lot of times in the academic setting, so I loved the opportunity. – STEPHEN

As a college student in Ohio during a presidential election year, Stephanie had a chance to learn about politics firsthand, by joining the College Democrats.

>> It was a tough loss, but it was such an awesome opportunity to be involved in campaigning. It was just undescribable, to be behind something with all your heart—we went to see John Kerry together, and things like that— and then, the letdown... That was definitely one of the best things that I did throughout my college years. – STEPHANIE

She found herself changing her own political beliefs, too, through her college experiences at college.

» I'm a lot more liberal now. I'm not saying I was really conservative in high school, but now my mind is more open to a lot of different things. Like this past summer, where I worked, a lot of gay guys work there. And now I almost get offended when someone else says something about a gay guy—I get upset. College is a great way to open your mind. - STEPHANIE

As Karen grew more active in the Native American association on campus, she also developed leadership skills she didn't know she had.

» One day I got tired of saying, "We're going to do this, we're going to do that," when we don't do nothing! I said, "Let's sit down right now, let's have a talk." I got out a piece of paper and I put down all the ingredients and I said, "What can you donate," and I set a time and a date, and I said, "I will call"—and right after that meeting, I called. - KAREN

Your social network also provides an emotional safety net.

At times, the difficulties of college life come at you like a flood, and friends know what you are going through better than anyone. After dropping out of high school, Hazel returned to earn her diploma through a special program that combined high school with community college. While she often needed a sympathetic ear, she didn't want certain people to worry.

» If I found myself struggling or needing help, I ran straight to friends that are about my age or a little bit older. I didn't want parents or teachers to know that I was having a hard time with my schoolwork, I thought that they would freak out and think that I was dropping out again. Anything but that! Instead, I would get pretty good advice from friends who had been in this situation before. - HAZEL

Karen finds supportive friendships in the Native American sorority at Oklahoma State, and Stephen found the same thing in a Latino fraternity at the University of Texas.

» I never thought I would be in a sorority! It's all Native women, to provide sisterhood for the college student. We're a social sorority, and we do a lot of community service hours, and we're big on education also. - KAREN

>> A lot of my fraternity brothers are first-generation college students. They know what it was like to be Mexican, what it was like to grow up in a humble household and for your parents not to be able to support you in the ways they wanted to. They don't have a lot of the same motivations and pushes as white students, but they are very determined, and I really appreciate and respect that. – STEPHEN

Friends your own age are not the only place to turn. Teachers, employers, and other adults can also provide emotional support. Aileen kept her part-time job when she began community college, and the same supervisors who had helped her on her way to college also stand by her when she needs it now.

>> The operations manager is the first in her family to graduate college, and her parents were strict like mine. So she understands me, and sometimes when I am going crazy, I'm too stressed and I need somebody to talk to, I go to her. You need somebody older, somebody wiser to talk to. Somebody that will understand what you're going through. – AILEEN

Milenny's Italian professors made sure that she persisted even when she was discouraged.

>> A lot of other professors were scared to break that barrier with the students, but my Italian professors were encouraging. They tried to make me feel comfortable, they told me, "You can do it!" Little things like that, for me, made a big difference. – MILENNY

Even in places that you wouldn't expect, you will find friends to support you when you need it. Eric made friends with the workers in his dormitory, for example.

>> People ask me, "Why do you know the entire kitchen staff? Why do you know the janitors?" I'm like, "If you shut out people, you're going to be by yourself." These are people, too. When I run out of Deacon Dollars, they feed me: "Baby, go on back there and get you whatever you want." When our heater broke, the next day it was fixed. Across all lines, you never know who can help you in life. – ERIC

Don't forget old friends and loved ones when you need support.

Your friends who have seen you conquer other obstacles can give you a valuable boost when the college path gets difficult. If you feel like giving up, reach out to them for help.

At the lowest point in Eric's first semester, feeling humiliated by a professor's response to his work, he decided that college was not for him. He went back to his dorm room, packed a suitcase, and called a close friend from high school to say he was coming home.

» And she started laughing at me. I was like, "What is so freaking funny?" She's like, "Let me tell you something! I'm at work right now, busting my butt to get where you are, and you're going to let one professor bring you away from something you worked your butt off to get? You deserve to be there, and you're just going to give it up like that?" I was like, Wow. – ERIC

Aileen Rosario lived with her family when she started college at the community college near her home in Paterson, New Jersey. She worked at a part-time job and helped her mother with the household chores. With all the stresses her family faced, no one had much time to talk about how college was going for Aileen. But her boyfriend was going through the same thing, which helped them both to keep trying.

» I talk a lot with him about school, because we almost have the same background. He's the first to go to college in his family, and he has to pay out of his pocket. He talks to me about some classes he's taking that I took already, like psychology and sociology. We help each other, which is good, 'cause nobody asks him at his house, "How are you doing in school?"
– AILEEN

Jackie always had the sense that her parents were watching out for her stress level. Whenever she got discouraged, they cheered her on.

» I'll tell them, "I just don't understand, this class is so hard, and I'm thinking of dropping it." And they're like "No, don't give up, Jackie, you're smart and you've got to keep going. Just think about it, you're studying right now and you're going to make it through!" – JACKIE

Jackie was lucky to have such family support, but not every student does. In the next section, you will hear other suggestions for keeping your emotional balance and reducing your stress, at the same time that you are managing the academic demands of college.

Find ways to take care of yourself.

When you feel overwhelmed by everything you have to do, it helps to break down big challenges into small ones. As you look at your obstacles one by one, pay close attention to what makes each thing hard. If you can find just one small way to deal with it, you will make your next day a little more satisfying.

The students in this book had a number of different suggestions for doing this:

Take time for yourself. Mike Morris went far from his rural Mississippi home to attend college at Brigham Young University in Utah, which recruited him to play football. He found the culture there completely foreign, from social life to religion, geography, and climate. A quiet person who guards his privacy, he often regained his sense of balance in solitude.

>> I'm one of those guys who sometimes doesn't like to be around a lot of people. I just like to isolate myself away from people and be by myself. Sometimes when you're by yourself you understand things better. And people don't understand that. – MIKE

Pay attention when you feel sad or lonely. Eric Polk, too, went to college far from home, and Wake Forest University felt worlds apart from his familiar past. He used his own knowledge of himself to find ways to ease his sadness and isolation.

>> I am an expert in loneliness. I get homesick—and I get lonely for myself, when I feel out of touch with myself. The way I deal with it, I just try to be goal oriented, to do things that make me feel fulfilled in some way. I make a "to do" list, and crossing out something makes me feel good. Or I write poetry, or a song—just putting the frustration out on the piano. Even just talking to people. I try to keep a smile on my face. Sometimes I feel like you have to laugh to keep from crying. – ERIC

Think positive. At first, both Jackie and Maly struggled with their difficult academic courses. But each of them decided to take a more accepting attitude toward their stresses, and focus on the positive aspects of their learning experiences.

>> You've got to fight against your negative thoughts, like how I thought that I wouldn't be good enough or smart enough in college, or "Maybe I can't handle this." I gotta put those thoughts away, and take the perspective that "I own my college and it doesn't own me." - JACKIE

>> I stopped stressing, because thinking about it as me being dumb and trying to do every little thing was just not working for me at all. I just went with the flow. After the first year I just started doing better and kept doing better. And my junior and senior year I really got the hang of things. - MILENNY

Limit partying. Jackie had to remind herself that taking time to relax was an important element of succeeding in college.

>> That's how it is in school—it's a roller coaster. Sometimes you deal with bad situations, and sometimes it's better. What I found the best is trying to collect myself and not to worry, because worry is the worst thing I can do for myself. I'm just going to try as hard as I can with the time that I have. And then I'm going to try and find a balance in my life as well. Spend time with my boyfriend and my friends and my family, and have quality time with them—even if it's just for fifteen minutes. You gotta find the things that'll make you feel happy. - JACKIE

Hazel also found that taking time out with her friends reduced her general stress level. But the college party scene, she noticed, turned out to be a bad way to do it.

>> Drinking and partying, if done improperly, just adds more stress to school. If anything, it's less stressful to wake up in the morning and go to class without a hangover than to wake up in the morning with your underwear on the ceiling and your head is throbbing and you have to go to a class. - HAZEL

As Karen attended Oklahoma State, she too noticed how many students seemed to be dragged down by the drinking culture. Native American students like her, she decided, had too much to lose by doing that.

》 Books and beer does not mix. I learned that very quick. For any student, being away from the confines of mother and dad, it's very easy to get into that party-party-party group. And it's a chemical imbalance that Natives have, they need to be aware that they might not have that alcohol tolerance. It's up to you to prioritize. Am I going to go to that party tonight, or am I going to study? Is your dream, what you want to be in life, more important, or is partying? Because partying will always be there; your dream will not always be there. – KAREN

Stephanie tried to hang out with people who cared about good grades as well as good times.

》 A lot of people think that college is all partying. I'm not saying that you shouldn't go out and party, because everyone does. Your friends are a major part of college, and obviously that's awesome, it's a good time. But the friends that I hang out with most, we like to go out, but if we have a test tomorrow, there's no way we're going to go out. – STEPHANIE

Get exercise. Jackie knew from experience that physical exercise helped relieve her stress levels, and she made it a priority. She signed up for a workout class on campus every semester, for elective credit, and she took every chance she got to play sports.

》 I love to play sports—it's a way to vent my stresses in a positive way, instead of going and partying on the weekend. It's a lot better because you feel great afterwards, and during, you're having fun. I'm a person who loves to interact with other people, and working out in a group makes me happy. And you don't have a hangover, that's for sure! – JACKIE

Enjoy the arts. Music, dance, art shows, and other artistic pursuits can also provide a good way to relieve your college stresses. At Northwestern University outside Chicago, Niema balanced her academic time by going out to the events that made her happy, from poetry slams to art shows.

Naixing, in San Francisco, decided to take a studio art class just for the pleasure and relaxation it gave him.

>> There are events every weekend, clubs you can go to, or museums. Anywhere you go, there's going to be something you can get into. Somewhere where you can find an outlet and you can find some type of joy. – NIEMA

>> I like to draw, and my friend was taking it, too. So I said to myself to take the art class, to enjoy it and also to strengthen our friendship. – NAIXING

Take breaks. If you feel discouraged by the academic challenges of college, taking a break from your books can lend you a fresh perspective. Joining a campus club, participating in a cultural or political event, trying out a new activity—all these count as part of your education, too. You'll take more energy, and more experience, back to your studies afterward.

>> I know a lot of people who feel like college sucks right now—but they're not leaving college. They're just not spending their whole life in the library. College has more to offer than books. – NIEMA

Get counseling. Sometimes college and personal issues will take an emotional toll that even your friends and family can't address. But feeling depressed does not reflect negatively on you, and your college has resources that can help you get better. Most campus health centers offer free counseling sessions that help you regain your balance.

Karen took advantage of this when family problems made it hard for her to concentrate on school.

>> There was a time where I thought my husband and I was going to split, and I could not study for a Spanish test. It helped when I went to university counseling. – KAREN

Maly definitely appreciated having a sympathetic ear when the stress got too great.

>> At first it was like, Well am I really at that point where I need counseling? So I went and tried it, and it was helpful. It's good to go and talk to somebody, even if they don't have the answer—especially when you're struggling

through finals and papers, and not losing your friends, staying in touch with family and not losing yourself. There is always that sense that your experience is very different from what anybody else is experiencing. But they understood. It's good to have somebody listen to you. – MALY

In coming to terms with her feelings of being an outsider, Maly was also developing a new sense of who she is and what she stands for.

>> I've grown very confident of what I believe in and what I am. Being in a very homogeneous college it's very easy to either go their way or completely isolate yourself from them. But I've learned how to stay in between—still participating in social events that they go to, but doing it in my own way. Always, always, stay true to yourself. – MALY

In the next chapter, others will tell more about how their sense of self developed as they went through college. As first-generation students, they faced issues of race, origin, social class, and economic privilege, and had to stay true to themselves while adapting to a whole new world.

WHERE TO GO FOR HELP

It helps to think about stress management *before* you are in the midst of a crisis. Use this space to write down the numbers of whatever resources your college or community may provide. Healthy stress relief comes in many forms—talk therapy, meditation, breathing exercises, physical activity—so make notes now about the things you would be most likely to try.

Your college counseling services: _____

Your college health center: _____

Your college fitness or recreation center _____

Classes available in stress management (these may include yoga, meditation, or other techniques):

_____

_____

_____

You can get free, confidential phone counseling and information by calling 24-hour telephone hotlines. Some helpful numbers are listed below, as well as contact information for other organizations that can provide information and resources in troubling situations.

National Mental Health Association Resource Center: 1-800-969-6642 (www.nmha.org)

Suicide Prevention Lifeline: 1-800-273-8255 (TTY users call 1-800-799-4889)

Suicide Prevention Hotline for Gay, Lesbian, Bisexual and Transgender Youth:
    1-800-850-8078 (www.thetrevorproject.org)

Sexually Transmitted Disease Information, Centers for Disease Control: 1-800-342-2437
    (www.cdc.gov)

Planned Parenthood, Inc.: 1-800-230-PLAN (1-800-230-7526)

Emergency Contraception Information: 1-888-NOT-2-LATE (1-888-668-2528)

National Alcohol and Substance Abuse Information Center: 1-800-784-6776
    (www.addictioncareoptions.com)

Relationship Violence Hotline: 1-800-799-SAFE (1-800-799-7233; TDD
    call 1-800-787-3224)

National Sexual Assault Hotline: 1-800-656-HOPE (1-800-656-4673)

Who Are You Now?

You develop a new identity while at college

*I*f **you didn't know his name,** Raja Fattah could pass as any kind
of inner-city student walking the bland suburban campus of Ohio's
Kent State University. The son of Palestinian immigrants, he grew up in a
poor black section of Cleveland and his tastes reflect the hip-hop culture.

>> I get it for being Puerto Rican, Mexican, black and white, Palestinian –
you can't tell what I am, so they're going to assume a lot of things, just
off the top. - RAJA

In Raja's years at college, for example, teachers have written him off as
unlikely to do well—before they saw his grade on the first test. His dorm
adviser has reported him for playing loud rap music, but ignored other
students who blast their rock and roll.

>> Just from little things like that, I knew that some people on this campus
didn't want to see people like me, people of my culture or background
or where I'm from or what I represent. That's just how it is. - RAJA

Inaccurate assumptions—by teachers, by fellow students, even by the
local police—have become an everyday fact of Raja's college career. But he
just keeps being himself: talking openly about discrimination, questioning
his own assumptions, having good times with friends, studying hard and
getting good grades, and working long hours at a gas station market to
pay for his education. Raja hopes for a job at the F.B.I. some day. If he gets
it, he will have had plenty of practice at moving through different cultures
and roles.

In this chapter, students describe the complicated and important
process of remaining true to themselves in an environment where they
differ from the norm. Just by getting to college, you have scaled a wall
that keeps thousands of capable and motivated students from higher
education because of their race, origin, social class, and access to money.

But confronting those issues does not stop once you are on the other side of the wall. And as you keep doing it, you will be forging a strong new identity.

Hold on to yourself.

Mingling with people in different college settings, many students have the chance to try on new roles or styles. Maly watched the fraternity and sorority scene at Lafayette College, and wondered where she fit in.

>> Being a freshman in college, I wanted to belong. And some people just want to belong so bad they would just follow the big groups. – MALY

Freedom to experiment with your identity can feel liberating. But make sure your choices reflect your values and character, shaped by the experiences unique to you. Eric signed up for a dorm where everyone agreed to stay away from using drugs, alcohol, or tobacco.

>> I really hate that my mom smokes. And there's a number of alcoholics in our family. I've been around the stuff all my life at home, I don't want to be around it at college! College is one of those things where you find yourself. It's about knowing who I am, but being able to be that person. I found out what Eric Polk would tolerate and what Eric Polk won't tolerate, what I will get involved with and what I won't. – ERIC

Both Eric and Jackie fought their way to college from high schools that gave them an academic preparation far below what they needed. They knew that others would be watching whether they could make the grade. But they had done it before, and they would do it now.

>> Do not forget where you come from. When you get to college and you finally taste that freedom, don't forget the struggles that brought you where you are. All the frustration that you had, all the times where you felt like you're not going to make it, and how you found that motivation to go ahead and do it anyway. You're lost if you forget it, you're lost. – ERIC

>> We all represent our groups—no matter what we do, our actions, or lack of action, will show it. I found ways to take pride in my culture and to feel

confident in that, without having to worry about what other people think. By succeeding in school, I am representing my group in a good way. - JACKIE

You can teach other students by being real about who you are.

Eric felt uncomfortable when his rich white friends wanted to borrow his clothes for a "ghetto" party. So he spoke up.

» For people out here who don't know the reality of growing up in the ghetto, it's my responsibility to share that. It's not a game—that's everyday life for some people. For you to play around with it because you don't know any better, that's fine, but if I'm here to explain it, I don't expect to see that coming from you again. Because that's offensive. So now it's like, "Dang, Eric, you really got outspoken." - ERIC

It bothered Milenny to see other students acting as if money didn't matter.

» If I used a napkin to dry my hand, I put it on the side so that it could dry. My roommate would take five napkins to clean a mirror, and I was like, "You just need one!" For me, you don't throw anything away—if you can't use it, someone else can! Over the years, [my roommate] learned a lot more. But some people just throw money away, and that was really strange to me. They would go out and buy five pairs of jeans, and I was like, "Okay! You will waste your money!" - MILENNY

Like Eric and Milenny, you have a lot to contribute to other people's knowledge and understanding, in your conversations with them about race, origin, class, and money. Though such discussions are rarely easy, everybody learns from them.

» A lot of people here have led sheltered lives—even now, they do. They grew up where it's easy to get away from people not like them, to only see rich white people that look just like themselves. And sometimes it causes heat, for me to say things from what I know about the world. It's not as sheltered as they think it is! I'm not going to be fake with anybody, I want to be as real as I possibly can. Sometimes they teach me stuff, sometimes I teach them stuff. I mean, that's college for you. - ERIC

Speak out if people stereotype you or others.

People often deal with social discomfort by trying to be funny. But you don't need to laugh it off if people make jokes about your background or disrespect where you're coming from. At first, Milenny responded politely to people who crossed the line.

>> One of my friends said, "You probably live in a ghetto neighborhood." I said, "Yeah, I think if you would go there, you would consider it ghetto." – MILENNY

But later she grew impatient with the ignorance reflected in such stereotypes.

>> We went out to eat in Providence, in this area with a lots of Hispanics and minorities, and she was scared, like, "I'm gonna die, they're gonna hit me with a car!" I was like, "No they're not, they're just people!" – MILENNY

Eric also got tired of playing along with certain attitudes. He decided that from now on he would stand up for his identity.

>> At first, I would go along with "you're ghetto." I was like, "I sure am from the projects!" —making a joke of something that I really took to be very serious. And that was not cool, just to go along with it. It feeds into that stereotype. I can't do that to you all who were raised up like me. So I don't play around with those racial jokes no more. If I'm going to be here and learn, if I'm going to accept different cultures and different styles, then you all gotta be at least a little respective and acceptive to what I bring. – ERIC

Stephen had to defend himself as a Mexican-American soon after he started at the University of Texas. He had worked hard to get there, and he knew he could handle the academics. But he discovered that some people had different opinions.

>> There are students here from across the country, across the world, and across this huge state, who aren't necessarily going to respect you for who you are. Some people are going to assume that you are here because of affirmative action, that your merit doesn't warrant you to be in this position. Do incoming students have the support and the resources to withstand an experience like that? – STEPHEN

Stephen began to provide that support for fellow students, through the university's Latino Leadership Council.

Find places to talk openly with other students about identity.

At her mostly white state university in Ohio, Stephanie's course in Latino studies was the first place she felt comfortable talking in a mixed group about race and ethnicity.

》 It was cool, because everyone was speaking their mind, and the minority in that class was Caucasian people. It definitely helped you feel like you're not leaving your people behind. Maybe we [Latinos] didn't all come from the exact same background, but we pretty much felt the same way about different things we talked about in class. Which is really different, and it opened up the eyes of the white kids in the class. - STEPHANIE

With a skilled teacher, a class like that can provide a safe place to explore issues of identity and to directly investigate the history of a culture. Multicultural centers or clubs offer the same advantage, in a less formal setting.

》 The international students association is by far the best organization on campus. They're so welcoming, everybody's integrating, it's not just about one culture or one person. We're learning about everybody, we're learning about everything. - MALY

Have a plan for how to respond if you encounter prejudice.

Race and class prejudices exist, even on liberal college campuses. Students of color, working-class students, women, and gay and lesbian students commonly experience the kind of bias that Raja encountered in many of his classes.

》 Some of the teachers look at me and they figure, "This guy is a clown, he's not here to learn. He looks like he's urban, his pants are sagging, he's got his hat on backward," or something. They're going to look at what you wear and how you're walking and they're basically going to judge your personality on that. That's the main thing I had to get over—every year, every semester, half my classes were this way. Basically, I just had to get a A on their test so they'll know that I'm not a clown. - RAJA

As Raja discovered, your good academic performance in school can help you push back against the prejudices that others hold about you. But the law is also on your side. If you feel you have experienced discrimination on campus—whether in class, the dining hall, or your residence—you have the right to bring it to the attention of someone in charge.

Every college has a non-discrimination policy as well as a dean or other official whose job is to address and resolve such issues and complaints. When you bring them to light, you are helping the college move forward. Slurs and derogatory or discriminatory language about anyone are not acceptable in a learning environment.

Stay open to the new things you see.

Even as he experienced the problems of looking and acting different, Raja also enjoyed standing out from the crowd. He began to notice variety of all kinds among his fellow students.

》 My campus has got 30,000 people on it, so when you're walking to class, you're walking within five, six thousand people. Some sense inside of you wants to be different from others. And you are different—everybody's different, no matter where you're from. - RAJA

Part of his education, he realized, was to explore the mix of people around him, discovering who they were and making a place for himself at college. If he changed along the way, that was also a way of growing.

》 If you're gonna go to any school, you just have to have an open mind about where you're going. You can't go in there thinking, "What if they don't like me?" A bunch of "what ifs" is going to end up in nothing. You'll always find a group of people that have your same interests, that are there to learn and to have fun and enjoy it, just like you. That's the biggest thing to get over. - RAJA

You can learn a lot by getting to know people whose experiences do not match yours. Raised in a churchgoing African-American family, Eric tried not to judge people he met whose lives were very different from his.

》 Being around people that are openly gay, it shocked the heck out of me. But if you come to college with a closed mind, you're not going to get very far.

College is a place for you to grow, not just academically. You grow socially, you grow emotionally, you grow spiritually. You can't come to college and not try to be receptive to everything else that's going on around you. You don't have to do what other people are doing, you just tolerate what people do. – ERIC

Many students feel shy at the idea of making friends with people who seem to have little in common with them. At his largely Mormon university in Utah, Mike kept to himself at first. But he began to enjoy seeing how people acted in this place whose customs were so different from his Mississippi ways.

» Back home, our parties go till about two or three in the morning, and there's drinking, smoking, fighting, all of the above! Here, parties end at twelve, and no drinking. The way people move is very different, like they're dancing sometimes with an off-beat. You don't see break-dancing where I'm from. All that is kind of interesting to me. – MIKE

Your college experiences—from courses to late-night discussions—might cause you to rethink your own beliefs or opinions. Although Stephen deeply identified with his church community in high school, he found his ideas about religion shifting during his college years. He still considers himself a Christian, but he rejects the political groups that often claim that label.

» I know what I believe in strongly, but I don't feel like church is a place where I can be me in the best of ways. My mom always said, "You can do anything you want during the week, but come Sunday morning, you give your time to God." And that's something I strongly believed in. But it's hard for me to identify with a community that uses hate in any kind of way. It's hard. – STEPHEN

Many people who go away to college like their new environment so much that they want to stay in the area after graduation. John likes to joke about his "redneck" rural background, but he realizes how much college has changed his preferences.

>> Now my personal preference is to live in a larger urban environment. That's just where I feel more comfortable—to be out in the country for two days drives me insane! I'll spend the afternoon in Indianapolis at museums and walking around town, just to give me something to do, just to give my mind a break, something to process, rather than just watching the horses running across outside the window as my nephew takes a nap. – JOHN

Milenny plans to eventually return to New York City, but first she wants to see more of the world.

>> For me, going away was more of a learning experience than probably almost everything I learned in college. You learn more about life than about academics. I feel like if I had to encourage a person to go to college I would tell her to leave [home.] It makes you reflect on your experiences here when you come back. I remember coming back and just seeing everything so differently. – MILENNY

From now on, you'll move in and out of different roles and cultures.

Staying true to yourself will sometimes mean changing, but it also includes remembering your roots. Your college education makes you something of a "shape-shifter"—you know what the old settings call for, as well as the new ones. You'll be equipped to move in and out of different cultures all the time—a rare gift.

In a college where nobody else dressed like him, Eric tried to fit in but still hold on to his own style.

>> I had never worn khakis in my life. I would come to class in saggy jeans, with a do-rag on and a cap turned to the side and tenderloin boots. But then I found out I could buy four pairs of khakis for what I would pay for one jeans outfit. So now I'm mixing both of them. My earrings and my necklace—this is me. It's not being white, it's not being black, it's embracing hip-hop culture and it's embracing another culture. – ERIC

Niema went home to Oakland for her first winter break, and she felt right away how much she had changed.

» You think, "Oh, when I come back I won't be that different." But so many different experiences happen in college, and you do grow up a lot. By the first week back home, I missed college! I was sending emails and calling and facebooking people, "Oh, I miss you with all my life! I can't wait to get back home!" People get mad: "Did you just call Evanston home?!" Well, that's where my life is, that's where all my friends are right now — yeah, Evanston's home! - NIEMA

Niema is describing the dilemma that almost all college students must deal with—resolving who they are now, in relation to the folks back home. As you walk that bridge, you find a new self is emerging, more interesting than ever. In the next chapter, students talk of how they stayed connected to the people and places they came from, while allowing new growth and changes to take place.

BUILDING MY RESUME

As your sense of identity develops and matures, so will your ideas about what to do for your work. When the time comes, your college's career services office can help you format your resume. To start, however, you will need a record of your experiences and accomplishments. Use this worksheet to write down (and update) what you do each term.

Have you belonged to any student organizations? List them here, along with any positions you held or projects you participated in.

Organization _____ Dates _____

Your Activities/Position _____

Organization _____ Dates _____

Your Activities/Position _____

Have you been involved in any community organizations or volunteer work? List them here.

Organization _____ Dates _____

Your Activities/Position _____

Your Supervisor _____

Organization _____ Dates _____

Your Activities/Position _____

Your Supervisor _____

Have you worked at an internship or job? Write the details here.

Organization _____ Dates _____

Position/What You Did _____

Your Supervisor_____

Organization _____ Dates _____

Position/What You Did _____

Your Supervisor_____

TIP Your positive experiences on the job can turn into good recommendations later. When you leave any position, ask your supervisor if you can give their name when you are applying for future opportunities (in work or further education).

Have you recently received any honors or awards, or had any other note-worthy achievements? If so, write them here:

_____

_____

What skills and interests have you developed? List them here:

Languages: _____

Computer Skills: _____

Sports: _____

Arts: _____

Other Interests:_____

9

Reaching Back Home

Will your family and friends change, too?

When she was in high school, Milenny Then argued with her parents about her plan to leave their Dominican neighborhood in New York City and go away to college in Massachusetts.

>> I was tired of being home, and my mother wanted to keep me in the house. Finally I said, "All right, then, I'm not coming back till I graduate, and you'll see that I'm not crazy." – MILENNY

Milenny did come back home often, once she was in college, but she also kept branching out into a wider world. She went to Italy to study for the spring semester of her junior year. After graduation, she was accepted into the Teach for America program in Atlanta, Georgia. On visits home, she frequently had to defend her choices to her large extended family and her friends from the neighborhood.

>> Now that I'm going away to Atlanta, they're like, "That's so far, why do you have to leave again?" I think it's really hard for them to accept that I'm willing to do anything once. A lot of people don't do those things because of fear. But I'm young, I don't have anything to tie me to one place right now. – MILENNY

Even though Milenny pushed back against her family's wishes, their relationship has stayed strong. She knows her parents are motivated by love for her. So while she established her independence and made plans for her future, she kept up her close connections with family and friends. To her surprise, people back home are changing, too.

You may be like Milenny, with a family that hovers over your shoulder. Or you might recognize yourself in Debra, who had no one on her side and went through the college experience alone.

> ›› I was the adult in my house. There was no one in my life who was telling me, "You can do this, you are capable of doing this." – DEBRA

Wherever you fit on this spectrum, your relationships with the people back home will no doubt shift in many ways during your college years. In this chapter, students describe how such changes—even though they might not be easy—can have a positive effect on all of you.

Accept your parents for who they are.

As you learn all kinds of new things in college, it's normal to start evaluating or criticizing the attitudes of the family you came from. But at a certain point, you may also recognize that the older generation is unlikely to "grow out of" long-held values or habits.

> ›› I think my family has changed a lot since I went to college. They're more open-minded now, they're more accepting of what I do, and they have more knowledge than before. But for the most part, they haven't changed in the way they want me to *be*, they don't want me to go out, they don't want me to go far. That's how they were raised and how their parents were, and they're just never going to change. – MILENNY

Milenny didn't like it when her parents insisted on calling her every single day throughout her college years. But eventually she accepted that their need to check on her well-being could not be changed.

> ›› My mother would get upset because I wouldn't tell her stories about my day. There was nothing to say! I ate, I went to class, I did regular things. Same thing as yesterday! Some of my relatives spoke to her and said, "She has a lot of work, she's going to be rude to you because she's stressed, so you should leave her alone." So she tried to stop, but it didn't work. – MILENNY

Find ways to keep in touch with home that work for you.

Niema is very close to her mother, but she doesn't have time for the daily phone calls they too used to have. In her first year at college, she found other ways to stay in steady contact with her parents.

» I don't talk to her as much, but when we do talk, it's for very long. We instant message each other, so there's never a lack of communication. I never exactly talked nonstop to my pops, but now he's learning how to use instant messaging, because he knows I'm always on it. He'll tell me what book I should be reading, because we're into different types of books. – NIEMA

To keep her grandmother connected with what she was doing, Niema once sent an envelope of clippings from her campus newspaper.

» And she leaves this phone message: "Pumpkin, it's Granny! I got your articles, I'm just so proud of you in college! Okay, have fun studying! Goodbye!" She didn't even mind that I couldn't talk to her, so that was really reassuring. – NIEMA

If your family members do not reach out to connect with you, they may need some encouragement. You could supply them with stamped envelopes and address labels with your college address, for example, or give them a reminder sheet to post on the fridge, with your phone number and the best times for them to call. (See the example at the end of this chapter.) If you wish you heard from home more, say so.

» Sometimes you just have to tell your parents, "You're not calling enough." I think people have pride issues. But sometimes you do need your parents to call you. If I get in a bad mood I don't want to talk to anybody but my mommy. – NIEMA

You don't have to lose friends who didn't go to college.

When you choose college, you may be leaving behind friends whose lives will go in another direction. But those old relationships do not have to end. They can even lend you support.

» None of my friends are in college right now, but they all like that I am. They're like, "Oh, there's our college girl!" – HAZEL

» I've been friends with the same person since I was in first grade, and I still talk to him. He dropped out of high school in tenth grade, and he has a child now. When I'm at home, he's telling me, "Keep doing what you're doing so you don't have to struggle like this." So in a way that's a support. – NIEMA

On their breaks from school, Niema and Raja still connect easily with old friends.

>> It's good to have these newfound experiences that you can share with them. Certain things that I study, they have no idea what I'm talking about, and it's just like, "Uh, take that away from me!" But I discuss poetry with certain people who are into poetry. And they tell me all the things that I've been missing out on in the neighborhood. – NIEMA

>> There's so much other problems in some of their lives, they're not worried about whether me coming out of college is going to affect how they're going to act towards me. They're all happy for me, though, that I went through the whole four years. Where I'm from, a lot of people think four years is a long time to do anything. – RAJA

When Stephen sees friends from his high school football team, or stops by to see an old teacher or coach, he still experiences a rush of memories.

>> The relationships I developed on the field were ones that you don't find a lot of places. It's not the teamwork that people expect of you in engineering or business, but it's a teamwork of something else. The guys I played with are still my best friends, we still call each other up and hang out. A while back, we were walking down 6th Street, and we started walking in the order that we lined up on the field. We had a great community of teachers and people who really cared, and if I go back for homecoming and things like that, I still make sure to go by and say hello and keep in contact to a certain extent. – STEPHEN

It can be hard to explain your new perspectives to those who haven't been there.

As Milenny and Eric discovered, some of your new interests may separate you from those back home. Expect new tensions as well as pleasures.

>> There's less for us to talk about, because my life revolves around school. And some of the things I'm learning, they just wouldn't understand. My parents couldn't tell you what sociology was about, they were never

exposed to anything like that. I can't get into anything really in depth, like politics and religion. My family would be sitting there going, "Huh?" - JOHN

>> I'm different from everybody in my family, in every single way. I know they can't relate to me and they don't know what I'm going through. It makes me angry with them. It's like, "Oh I can't talk to nobody in this house!" - AILEEN

Your parents might want to talk about the time and money your college education requires, more than about what you are learning.

>> I never have talked to them about what I actually am doing or what I'm actually trying to do in college. I just tell them I want to be a lawyer. This is the one question they always ask me: "How long is it going to take you?" I tell them eight years, and that's it. End of conversation. - AILEEN

Keep talking to your family about college, even if it seems like they can't relate.

At times, you may conclude those at home cannot possibly understand your experiences at college. But tell them whatever you can. You are making an important emotional connection when you talk to them about your new life.

>> My twin sister seems to understand me more than anybody else, because she really listens. But does she understand what it's like for me to have to get up at seven forty-five, be in class by nine, go through my full day, and still be up till one or two in the morning getting my homework done? No. - JOHN

>> It makes my mother sad in a way, because her daughter can't come talk to her. But she's really happy that I can talk to [my supervisors] at work! So instead of asking her for advice, I explain to my mother the things that they tell me. - AILEEN

You could find that people at home connect in different ways to what you're learning. For example, Naixing likes to tell his parents some things about his Asian studies class, but not everything.

>> I do not feel comfortable sharing with my family the negative experiences that Asian Americans went through in the United States. I only share the

achievements they gained, like how Chinese labor helped lay the transcontinental railroad in amazingly fast speed. – NAIXING

Sometimes you might decide not to give details about certain aspects of your life at college. Naixing and Aileen know their parents have enormous burdens already, so they try to keep private the stress they feel.

» Sometimes when I do not do well on specific exams, I keep it a secret. When I have too much work or pressure, I usually keep it to myself, and also when other things are happening with my family. When my grandmother was sick, that sadness added to my pressure, and sometimes it made me cry. I talked with my parents but they did not seem to understand. – NAIXING

» I wouldn't talk to my family about what a class requires of me. I tell them I'm doing good, but if I'm doing bad I won't tell them. If I fail the first test, I just try to do better the next time. – AILEEN

With her sisters at home, however, Aileen sometimes finds herself having a different kind of conversation than before, about the new ideas that she is studying.

» I talk to them more about things I learn in school, and how it does relate to how we live or what we do, why things happen or why things shouldn't happen. – AILEEN

You are an inspiration to your family and friends.

One of the satisfactions of going to college is watching other people's lives change because they see you doing well. The pride they take in you can turn into new ambitions for themselves.

» My older brother's the one that told me, plain and simple, to go to college —instead of just working nine to five every day with no advancement. He's thirty years old right now. And it's a funny situation, because after two years of me going, he finally went to college, like ten years after graduating from high school. – RAJA

>> When I'm doing good, my parents tell me that I encourage them. My mom gets exams at work, too, because where she works you have to know what you're doing. So she'll come home: "Look, Jackie, I got 100 percent!"
– JACKIE

>> My mom's bored with her job, so she's thinking about going and taking some classes. She says things like, "Maybe we'll graduate at the same time!" – NIEMA

Niema likes to visit her high school in Oakland, from which few students go on to college. When she talks to younger people about their possible futures, she knows that her example is giving them hope.

>> A lot of people where I'm from, this is their only opportunity to find out about college! – NIEMA

Time away gives you a new perspective on your home environment.

You may feel more critical of the place you came from, when you return to it from college—or you may feel more understanding. Niema, for instance, realized just how stressful her high school social life had been.

>> At parties in college, I don't have to worry about the party getting busted up by the cops, or somebody wanting to shoot somebody for talking to somebody else's girlfriend. I was trying to explain to a friend back home the freedom in going to a party and not being, like, "I wonder if that dude's got a gun?" And she was like, "What? Are you serious?" She couldn't grasp that. NIEMA

Stephen wonders if he has the right to judge his father's point of view.

>> He's a great guy, but his conversation is only with whoever walks into his barbershop. He doesn't understand the discussions of race or gay rights, the political debates that come up on the news. It's hard to determine if I want to initiate the effort, or if, as a fifty-year-old man, he's solid in what he believes in. Do I have a right to say, "These are things you need to think about?" He's lived on this earth a lot longer, and his reality isn't mine.
– STEPHEN

Aileen's academic studies have made her think differently about her family and how they behave.

》 I took a psychology course about human growth and development, from the womb to your death. And it made me look at my three nephews that live in my house in a certain way: "Oh, that's why he does this!" It makes me think about everybody in our house and the things they do, the things they say. – AILEEN

Raja has developed even more respect for the values his mother and father hold dear.

》 My father's more educated than I am, and he's never been past high school. He's always taught himself, and he speaks five languages. My mother is the same way. They always look at me like, "You've accomplished something, but this is not the end. You still have to go out there and make it for your-self and start your own family." – RAJA

Seeing people from home can feel bittersweet.

Once Hazel went back to school, she had to cut back on her social life with old friends.

》 I used to love hanging out with my tight circle of friends. We would go out to midnight movies, bowling, dinner, and most of it took place late at night. Cutting that much time out of our lives hanging out together really had an impact. I was out of the loop, and that made me sad. – HAZEL

As an older student, John also sees that his friends have different priorities now.

》 Most of my friends have their families already established, they're busy taking their kids to soccer practice or this place and that place. The ones that I do keep up with live in different places, so I don't see them much. – JOHN

Stephanie still hangs out sometimes with friends from her old neighborhood. But it reminds her of the growing distance that college has put between them.

>> I'm always trying to do both—be with my friends from college and friends from my neighborhood. But when I talk to friends from the neighborhood, or my cousin even, it's more along the lines of "So-and-so is in jail." It's not that I can't talk about that kind of stuff, but it's a good reminder of "You don't want that." – STEPHANIE

For Eric, going home to his old neighborhood can bring news of desperate sadness.

>> I had a really good group of eight friends. When I got back this summer, there were only two left. Two are dead, one of them got shot to death. Three of them are fathers now. And those three plus one more are in jail. I saw the same things, smoking weed and getting high and getting drunk. They're men now, 21, 22, but they're living at home with their parents, not working. – ERIC

Having shared that kind of history, Eric treasures his relationships with the friends he has remaining. They still treat him like a hero, who's going out there for all of them.

>> One time I went back, there's five guys all sitting on the front of Dwayne's porch. The two guys that I knew ran up and gave me a hug and whatnot, and they introduced me to the others and the guy goes to pass me the joint. And my friend is like, "What? No, he don't smoke, you can't let him have that!" It made me smile, the memory—I was home again. – ERIC

You might also leave people behind.

Not everyone has friends as supportive as Eric's, and no one has time to keep up every relationship. Some of your other friendships will probably have to get less from you than they once did. Raja tries to see his relatives and friends back in Cleveland, but between his job and his studies he cannot manage to visit as often as he wishes.

>> I had a lot of friends growing up and over a hundred cousins, and we used to all hang out. I still associate with all of them, but it's hard to find time. You just have to live with that—everybody moves on to different roads, and some people might be just too far down the road. You grow out of that whole life you had when you was eighteen years old. – RAJA

Hazel's relationship with her boyfriend changed a lot when she started college, and eventually they broke up.

>> I couldn't go and see him as much, and he totally hated it. He wanted me to drop out of school. Now I've been trying to surround myself with people who understand that this is what I want to do. And this really makes me happy, what I'm doing. – HAZEL

Sad things at home may affect your path at college.

Partly because Mike went to college in order to better support his family some day, he is always thinking about their welfare when he is away at school. If things go wrong at home, he finds it especially difficult to be far from home.

>> Most of the time they don't call me to tell me bad news, because they know I'll be wanting to leave school and go home. My sister was put in jail, and there was nothing I could do, really. And just recently, my cousin's grand-daddy died. He used to whup me, feed me, take care of me, and I didn't have a chance to go home to the funeral. – MIKE

In Naixing's Chinese family, his grandmother held the traditional place of honor. When she fell ill during his first summer in college, his parents were working long restaurant hours. It was a hard decision, but Naixing dropped his English composition class to care for her.

>> If I dropped the course, I could take it again another semester. But I only have only one grandma, and I could not leave her unattended. I did not consult my parents, because I knew that they would tell me to keep the class and hand over the duty of taking care of my grandmother to them. – NAIXING

You might, on the other hand, have to make the hard decision to put your education before your role at home. If this happens to you, remember that you honor your family by developing your full potential.

Going home will make you notice how you have changed and grown.

In both good ways and hard ways, going back home will show you how things are changing. Niema's relationship with her parents relaxed and matured, for example.

》 You come back and there's like a calmness, a new layer to your relationship, because you had that space. There's been time for your parents to deal with the fact that you're not a baby anymore. - NIEMA

But the changes can also make you feel uncomfortable. When Milenny put on her new platform flip-flops to go out with her brother, he told her to change her shoes.

》 He was like, "I'm not going outside with you in those—you look like a white girl!" And I said, "But I like them!" And he's like, "No-no-no, change them!" So I was like, "Fine." I didn't care after a while, but at first it was hard to deal with that. Just little things—the way I spoke, the way I dressed, they were like, "Hmmm, you're acting different, why are you acting strange?" - MILENNY

Eric's cousin felt threatened by his new vocabulary—and by his worldview, which was less black-and-white than before.

》 We went to the mall and there was this white guy who had on this do-rag and his pants sagging. My cousin was like, "That's such a typical white guy. I don't understand why he wants to be black." I was like, "I don't think he wants to be black, I think he just wants to embrace the hip-hop culture. You sound pretty biased." He's like, "What's that mean?" I'm like, "Like you have a prejudice towards people." He's like, "Don't be using no big words with me!" I was like, "That's not a big word!" - ERIC

You will always be gaining new insight about your relationships with the people back home, and learning new ways to connect with the people you love. Because they provided your first sense of who you were, they will continue to matter, even as you grow and change. It's not easy to keep the right balance, as Milenny says:

》 It's just been hard really dealing with them and trying to remain normal to them and normal to myself! - MILENNY

But you can be sure it's worth the trouble.

STAYING CONNECTED WITH FAMILY

Once you know your college schedule and your contact information, fill out the worksheet on the opposite page and ask your family to put it on the refrigerator or near the phone. They can use it to keep in touch, to let other people know how to reach you, to send "care packages" from home at stressful times, or just to know a little more about your life away at college.

TIP Getting mail when you are away at college feels wonderful! Leave your friends and family with labels that have your college address already written on them, to make it easy for them to send you things. (Write the address on the lines below, or use your computer to print out the labels.)

How (and When!) to Keep in Touch with Me

My phone number(s): _____

_____

My email address: _____

_____

My mailing address: _____

_____

Name(s) of my roommate(s): _____

_____

Good times of day or week to call me: _____

_____

Please don't call me at these times: _____

_____

I have final exams during this time period: _____

_____

I have a winter break during this time period: _____

_____

I have a spring break during this time period: _____

_____

Don't forget how much I need and miss my family!

10

Pass It Forward

You'll help those who follow you

So many of the students in this book have already started to help others follow in their footsteps to college. Niema goes back to Oakland to talk to classes at her old high school. Stephen runs workshops at the University of Texas that help Latino youth think about what moves them ahead and what holds them back. John has spoken at a conference for guidance counselors in Indiana. Milenny is going to teach high school in Atlanta, with Teach for America. Eric works in the same Nashville community agency that steered him to Wake Forest University.

Everyone has something to learn from you as a first-generation college student. You can teach people the unfairness of an educational system that stacks the cards against capable and motivated students like you. You can describe the obstacles they often face on the way to college: lack of financial support; inadequate academic preparation; and insufficient information, guidance, and encouragement. And you can show, with pride, what you are accomplishing against the odds.

Your hard work in the next few years will result in your college degree, and the rewards will follow. Just as important, your success will give confidence to many others that they can succeed in college, too. So don't forget the many concrete ways to show the world how much strength, determination, and intelligence you bring to your higher education. Here are just a few—you can add your own ideas to fill out the list.

- Go back to your high school and talk to students about your college experience.

- Visit the teachers and mentors who helped you get into college. Remind them how much it mattered that they cared about your future.

- Invite a prospective first-generation student to visit you on campus. That one experience can make a huge difference in whether college seems possible to someone.

- As you finish each college year, go see your college dean or faculty advisor to review your progress and to plan for the coming year. Speak honestly about your struggles, share your successes, and ask for advice.

- Plan now for what might come after college. What you do in the summer after each college year can connect you with a network of people who will know and value you, whether you go on to further study or into the workplace.

- Seek out people you admire who graduated from your college. Introduce yourself and let them know you are proud to attend the same school they did. Ask their advice on where to go with your college degree.

"I did college the hard way," said Debra Graves, who was already a working mother when she began her education again at a community college. "But eventually I will get into university."

》 And my dream for my boys is that they will go straight from high school to university. I'm most proud that, even though my sons may not recognize it now, the things I am doing now will have a huge impact on who they become as men. I don't need their recognition now. I just need to see them succeed at whatever efforts they take on. That will be enough recognition of me. Debra knows that her hard work has paved the way for her sons to follow. Your example, too, will make a difference to people you may never know. – DEBRA

Debra knows that her hard work has paved the way for her sons to follow. Your example, too, can make a difference to others, even if you never find out just who. Have pride, and pass it forward!

Useful Resources

Once you are enrolled in college, you will still need to consult outside resources to help you stay in, study effectively, pay your way, use your summers well, graduate, and go on to further study or work. Use the following list as a starting point from which you can track down websites containing the information you need.

PAYING FOR COLLEGE

www.studentaid.ed.gov
Available in English and Spanish, The Student Guide is a comprehensive resource on student financial aid from the U.S. Department of Education.

www.nacacnet.com
The National Association for College Admission Counseling provides this list of links to scholarships, lenders and other resources. Go to their "Online Resources" and then click on "financial aid."

www.collegeispossible.org
The College Is Possible website offers "Paying for College," an overview of federal grants and loans; tax benefits for college students; and other federal, state and institutional programs.

www.studentaid.org
The National Association of Student Financial Aid Administrators provides information on the financial aid process for students and parents. You can also download here an excellent document on what college students should know about credit card use.

www.fastweb.com
This free service from Monster.com allows users to search over 600,000 scholarships worth more than $1 billion.

www.irs.gov

If you are earning money while you are in college, you will most likely have to file tax returns. This Internal Revenue Service website offers help specifically for students; go to "Individuals" and then click on "Students" for the most useful pages.

MULTICULTURAL RESOURCES

www.nacacnet.com

A list of counseling and financial aid sources to assist students from various ethnic and cultural backgrounds, from the National Association for College Admission Counseling. Go to their "Online Resources" and then click on "Multicultural Resources."

www.chci.org

This website by the Congressional Hispanic Caucus Institute offers a great list of scholarships, opportunities, and youth organizations for Hispanic and other minority students. From the home page, click on "Education Center" and follow the link for "Educational Resources" or any others that interest you.

www.blackexcel.org

A comprehensive resource especially dedicated to African-American families and first-generation college students. The website includes detailed information about preparing for college, scholarships, historically black colleges (including virtual tours), and summer enrichment programs for high school minority students. There's also a free newsletter.

www.doorsofopportunity.org

A college student began this website listing summer opportunities for minority college students, and linking to other sites where you can explore even more.

The College Board website offers many useful tips on how to succeed in college. Go to www.collegeboard.com, then go to the "Students" section. Under the heading "Plan for College," click on "College Success" or go to this link: www.collegeboard.com/student/plan/college-success/index.html

All kinds of practical advice for college students appears in *The Ultimate College Survival Guide*, fourth edition, by Janet Farrar Worthington and Ronald T. Farrar (Lawrenceville, NJ: Peterson's Guides, 1998).

A reading and study method called SQR4 (standing for "survey, question, read, recite, rephrase, review") is worth learning to help you do better in your courses. It helps you "warm up your brain" for in-depth reading, identify important facts and concepts, understand how the information is related, and retain information in your memory. Type "SQR4" into your Internet search engine and you will find many links describing how it works.

CHANGING COLLEGES

If you find that the college you selected does not suit your needs and goals, you can apply to transfer to a different college. Research the other possibilities using the same resources that high school students use, below, but this time, fill out the application for transfer students. You will not need to retake the SAT or ACT exams, but your high school will have to send in your high school transcript, and your college will need to submit your college transcript so far. You will also need recommendations from college professors or deans (though not from your high school teachers). If you are thinking of transferring, it is even more important to work hard for good grades at your current college, and to make good relationships with professors who might recommend you.

www.collegeboard.com
The College Board website has tools for finding and applying to college. It offers a useful interactive tool called "My Organizer" that is well worth signing up for.

www.collegeispossible.org

A list of recommended websites, books and brochures from College Is Possible.

LIFE AFTER COLLEGE

www.gradschools.com

This is a comprehensive online source of information on graduate schools, sorted by subject area, geographical location, and other variables. It also includes useful information on graduate fellowships.

Graduate school admission exams

If you plan on applying to graduate school after you get your four-year college degree, you will have to take the Graduate Record Exams (GRE) or another standardized entrance test in a specialized field like law (the LSAT) , medicine (the MCAT), dentistry (DAT) or business (GMAT). For an overview of the different requirements, go to the following websites:

Graduate school, general: Educational Testing Service (www.ets.org)

Law school: Law School Admissions Council (www.lsac.org)

Medical school: Association of American Medical Colleges (www.aamc.org)

Dental school: American Dental Association (www.ada.org)

Business school: Graduate Management Admission Council (www.mba.com)

IMPORTANT DATES AND DEADLINES

Every college has a different schedule and different deadlines that you will need to remember. Use this worksheet to gather them, then transfer them all to your calendar.

Day to arrive at college: _____

First day of classes:

        Term 1 _____

        Term 2 _____

        Term 3 (if applicable)_____

Deadline to register for courses

        Term 1 _____

        Term 2 _____

        Term 3 (if applicable) _____

Deadline to drop courses without penalty

        Term 1 _____

        Term 2 _____

        Term 3 (if applicable)_____

TIP Write down on your planning calendar the dates of major tests and papers due in all your classes.

Thanksgiving break begins on:_____ and classes resume on:_____

Winter break begins on: _____and classes resume on:_____

Spring break begins on:_____ and classes resume on: _____

Exam period begins on:_____

Term 1 _____

Term 2 _____

Term 3 (if applicable) _____

Deadline for filing your federal taxes (both yours and those of your parent[s] are needed for financial aid, unless you are independent or your parents do not file taxes): _____

Deadline for Federal Application for Financial Aid (FAFSA, www.fafsa.ed.gov):

_____

Deadline for applying for financial aid (from your college):

_____

Deadline to file the CSS Profile form (if required by your college; see www.collegeboard.com): _____

Deadline to apply for dormitory or other college housing for following year:

_____

Graduation/Commencement day: _____

Other applications:

For summer internships or jobs _____

_____

For grants and fellowships _____

_____

For study abroad _____

_____

For other activities on or off campus _____

_____

MY YEARLY BUDGET

INCOME	
From your jobs	
From your parent(s) or guardian(s)	
From your student loans	
From your grants or scholarships	
From other sources	
INCOME SUBTOTAL:	
EXPENSES:	
Tuition and college fees	
Books	
Computer	
College room & board	
College meal plan (if separate)	
Rent (if living off campus)	
Utilities (if living off campus)	
Groceries	
Telephone	
Car payment	
Car insurance	
Gasoline, oil, maintenance	
Public transportation	
Health insurance (if separate from college fees)	
Personal care items	
Clothing	
Entertainment	
Eating out/snacks	
Miscellaneous expenses	
EXPENSES SUBTOTAL:	
NET INCOME: (Income less expenses)	

The student contributors

John Berry graduated from high school in rural Indiana. After working for several years, he entered Indiana/Purdue University at Fort Wayne, Indiana. He hopes to go on to graduate school and become a history professor.

Jackie Comminello began college at the University of Colorado at Denver, where she studied for two years. Then she transferred to the adjacent Community College of Denver, where she is pursuing a career in dentistry.

Raja Fattah lived in Palestine during his grade school years, then graduated from Max Hayes Vocational High School in Cleveland, Ohio. He worked his way through Kent State University, where he majored in justice studies.

Maly Fung attended a New York City public school for immigrant students. On a scholarship from the Posse Foundation, she attended Lafayette College in Easton, Pennsylvania, where she studied international relations.

Debra Graves left school in sixth grade, then completed a high school equivalency program. She was 26 and the mother of several boys when she enrolled at Denver Community College, and she plans to go on to earn her bachelors degree.

Hazel Janssen left her Denver high school before graduating. After two years in the labor market, she returned to Emily Griffith Opportunity High School, through which she also took community college courses at Denver Community College. She hopes for a career in the arts.

Niema Jordan graduated from Oakland Technical Arts High School in California. A student at Northwestern University in Evanston, Illinois, she plans a career in journalism.

Naixing Lei arrived from China at sixteen in San Francisco, where he began learning English in high school. He enrolled at City College of San Francisco, and will transfer to a four-year college to prepare for a career in business.

Mike Morris grew up in rural Mississippi, where he played football in high school. After studying for two years at a local community college, he transferred to Brigham Young University in Salt Lake City, Utah. He will major in recreational management and hopes to go on to a masters degree.

Eric Polk went to high school in Nashville, Tennessee, where he worked as a youth leader at Community Impact, a nonprofit neighborhood organization. Now at Wake Forest University in Winston-Salem, North Carolina, he belongs to a singing group and teaches hip-hop to other students.

Karen Powless combines her college studies with the responsibilities of marriage and children. She brings her young son with her to Oklahoma State University in Oklahoma City, where she is a leader in the Native American Students Association.

Rena Priest grew up on the Lummi Indian Reservation, near Bellingham, Washington. She attended Northwest Indian College and Western Washington University, and is now studying for her masters in fine arts at Sarah Lawrence College.

Aileen Rosario finished high school in Paterson, New Jersey, where she is an intern at the Paterson Education Fund. After two years at Passaic County Community College, she transferred to Montclair State University. She hopes for a career in law.

 Stephanie Serda grew up outside Toledo, Ohio, where after graduating from high school she enrolled at Bowling Green State University. There she studies sport management, works at a local YMCA, and is active with the College Democrats.

 Milenny Then graduated from Landmark High School in New York City. At Wheaton College in Massachusetts, her studies in Italian led her to spend a semester in Florence, Italy. She graduated in 2006 and is now a member of Teach for America.

 Stephen Torres grew up and graduated from high school in a rural area outside Austin, Texas. At the University of Texas in Austin, Texas, he was active in the Latino Leadership Council. He graduated in 2006 and began teaching in the Breakthrough Collaborative.